D1563024

Bio
Hornsby

BaT   12/06
RE

ROGERS HORNSBY

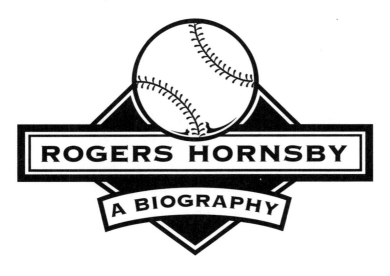

ROGERS HORNSBY

A BIOGRAPHY

JONATHAN D'AMORE

BASEBALL'S ALL-TIME GREATEST HITTERS

GREENWOOD PRESS
WESTPORT, CONNECTICUT • LONDON

Library of Congress Cataloging-in-Publication Data

D'Amore, Jonathan.
    Rogers Hornsby : a biography / Jonathan D'Amore.
      p. cm.—(Baseball's all-time greatest hitters)
    Includes bibliographical references and index.
    ISBN 0–313–32870–6 (alk. paper)
    1. Hornsby, Rogers, 1896–1963.   2. Baseball players—United States—Biography.
  I. Title. II. Series.
GV865.H6D43   2004
796.357'092—dc22   2004053047
[B]

British Library Cataloguing in Publication Data is available.

Library of Congress Catalog Card Number: 2004053047
ISBN: 0–313–32870–6

First published in 2004

Greenwood Press, 88 Post Road West, Westport, CT 06881
An imprint of Greenwood Publishing Group, Inc.
www.greenwood.com

Printed in the United States of America

The paper used in this book complies with the
Permanent Paper Standard issued by the National
Information Standards Organization (Z39.48–1984).

10 9 8 7 6 5 4 3 2 1

Every reasonable effort has been made to trace the owners of copyright materials in this book,
but in some instances this has proven impossible. The author and publisher will be glad to receive information leading to more complete acknowledgments in subsequent printings of the
book and in the meantime extend their apologies for any omissions.

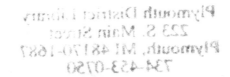

FOR MY BROTHER DANIEL,
THE BEST SECOND BASEMAN I KNOW.

People ask me what I do in the winter when there's no baseball.
I'll tell you what I do. I stare out the window and wait for spring.

—Rogers Hornsby, on the off-season

I don't know any other business and I don't want to.

—Rogers Hornsby, on baseball

CONTENTS

Contents

SERIES FOREWORD

The volumes in Greenwood's "Baseball's All-Time Greatest Hitters" series present the life stories of the players who, through their abilities to hit for average, for power, or for both, most helped their teams at the plate. Much thought was given to the players selected for inclusion in this series. In some cases, the selection of certain players was a given. **Ty Cobb**, **Rogers Hornsby**, and **Joe Jackson** hold the three highest career averages in baseball history: .367, .358, and .356, respectively. **Babe Ruth**, who single-handedly brought the sport out of its "dead ball" era and transformed baseball into a home-run hitters game, hit 714 home runs (a record that stood until 1974) while also hitting .342 over his career. **Lou Gehrig**, now known primarily as the man whose consecutive-games record Cal Ripken Jr. broke in 1995, hit .340 and knocked in more than 100 runs eleven seasons in a row, totaling 1,995 before his career was cut short by ALS. **Ted Williams**, the last man in either league to hit .400 or better in a season (.406 in 1941), is widely regarded as possibly the best hitter ever, a man whose fanatical dedication raised hitting to the level of both science and art.

Two players set career records that, for many, define the art of hitting. **Hank Aaron** set career records for home runs (755) and RBIs (2,297). He also maintained a .305 career average over twenty-three seasons, a remarkable feat for someone primarily known as a home-run hitter. **Pete Rose** had ten seasons with 200 or more hits and won three batting titles on his way to establishing his famous record of 4,256 career hits. Some critics have claimed that both players' records rest more on longevity than excellence. To that I would say there is something to be said about longevity and, in both cases, the player's excellence was the reason why he had the opportunity to keep playing, to keep tallying hits for his team. A base hit is the mark of a successful plate appearance; a home run is the apex of an at-bat. Accordingly, we could hardly have a series titled "Baseball's All-Time Greatest Hitters" without including the two men who set the career records in these categories.

Joe DiMaggio holds another famous mark: fifty-six consecutive games in which he obtained a base hit. Many have called this baseball's most unbreakable record. (The player who most closely approached that mark was Pete Rose, who hit safely in forty-four consecutive games in 1978.) In his thirteen seasons, DiMaggio hit .325 with 361 home runs and 1,537 RBI. This means he *averaged* 28 home runs and 118 RBIs per season. MVPs have been awarded to sluggers in various years with lesser stats than what DiMaggio achieved in an "average" season.

Because **Stan Musial** played his entire career with the Cardinals in St. Louis— once considered the western frontier of the baseball world in the days before baseball came to California—he did not receive the press of a DiMaggio. But Musial compiled a career average of .331, with 3,630 hits (ranking fourth all time) and 1,951 RBIs (fifth all time). His hitting prowess was so respected around the league that Brooklyn Dodgers fans once dubbed him "The Man," a nickname he still carries today.

Willie Mays was a player who made his fame in New York City and then helped usher baseball into the modern era when he moved with the Giants to San Francisco. Mays did everything well and with flair. His over-the-shoulder catch in the 1954 World Series was perhaps his most famous moment, but his hitting was how Mays most tormented his opponents. Over twenty-two seasons the "Say Hey Kid" hit .302 and belted 660 home runs.

Only four players have reached the 600-home-run milestone: Mays, Aaron, Ruth, and **Barry Bonds**, who achieved that feat in 2002. Bonds, the only active player included in this series, broke the single-season home-run record when he smashed 73 for the San Francisco Giants in 2001. In the 2002 National League Championship Series, St. Louis Cardinals pitchers were so leery of pitching to him that they walked him ten times in twenty-one plate appearances. In the World Series, the Anaheim Angels walked him thirteen times in thirty appearances. He finished the Series with a .471 batting average, an on-base percentage of .700, and a slugging percentage of 1.294.

As with most rankings, this series omits some great names. Jimmie Foxx, Tris Speaker, and Tony Gwynn would have battled for a hypothetical thirteenth volume. And it should be noted that this series focuses on players and their performance within Major League Baseball; otherwise, sluggers such as Josh Gibson from the Negro Leagues and Japan's Sadaharu Oh would have merited consideration.

There are names such as Cap Anson, Ed Delahanty, and Billy Hamilton who appear high up on the list of career batting average. However, a number of these players played during the late 1800s, when the rules of baseball were drastically different. For example, pitchers were not allowed to throw overhand until 1883, and foul balls weren't counted as strikes until 1901 (1903 in the American League). Such players as Anson and company undeniably were the stars of their day, but baseball has evolved greatly since then, into a game in which hitters must now cope with night games, relief pitchers, and split-fingered fastballs.

Ultimately, a list of the "greatest" anything is somewhat subjective, but Greenwood offers these players as twelve of the finest examples of hitters throughout history. Each volume focuses primarily on the playing career of the subject: his early years in school, his years in semi-pro and/or minor league baseball, his entrance into the majors, and his ascension to the status of a legendary hitter. But even with the greatest of players, baseball is only part of the story, so the player's life before and after baseball is given significant consideration. And because no one can exist in a vacuum, the authors often take care to recreate the cultural and historical contexts of the time—an approach that is especially relevant to the multidisciplinary ways in which sports are studied today.

Batter up.

ROB KIRKPATRICK
GREENWOOD PUBLISHING
FALL 2003

ACKNOWLEDGMENTS

Throughout the demanding and exciting experience of this project, I had the support of a large number of family members, friends, and acquaintances who were truly generous with their time, interest, and good wishes; I owe my gratitude to them all. I would like to thank the kind staffs at three excellent research facilities: the National Baseball Library, Cooperstown, New York; the *Sporting News* Archives, St. Louis, Missouri; and Davis Library at the University of North Carolina, Chapel Hill, North Carolina. Of particular help to the research and writing of Rogers Hornsby's life were Steven Gietschier, Jim Meier, Gabriel Schecter, Kevin O'Connor, Rob Kirkpatrick, and John Wagner.

I believe special thanks are due to my parents, David and Deborah D'Amore, who have been a constant source of love and support; to Bryan Pino, for honest readings of very rough drafts; to Bryan Sinche, whose encouragement at the beginning made the entire project possible; and to Maura McKee, a woman with great stores of intelligence, patience, and kindness, who supported my work on this book from its first to its final day.

CHRONOLOGY

1896 Born in Winters, Texas, on April 27 and named "Rogers" after his mother's family.

1898 His father, Aaron Edward Hornsby (b. 1857), dies in Runnels County, Texas, on December 17. His mother, Mary Dallas Rogers Hornsby, moves her five children to Rogers Hill, Texas.

1903 Mary Hornsby and her children move to Fort Worth, Texas, where her three older sons go to work in the booming meatpacking industry.

1914 Everett Hornsby, a minor league baseball player, arranges for his youngest brother to try out with the Dallas Steers of the Texas League. Rogers makes the team, but is released after two weeks without appearing in a game. He soon catches on with a Class D team in Hugo, Oklahoma.

1915 While playing for the Denison Railroaders of the Western Association, Hornsby gets the attention of Bob Connery, a scout for the St. Louis Cardinals. Connery purchases Hornsby's contract from Denison and sends him to play for the Cardinals and manager Miller Huggins. Hornsby makes his major league debut on September 10.

1916 Erasing Huggins' doubts by adding 20 pounds in the off-season, Hornsby hits well enough in spring training to earn a permanent place in the starting line-up. He hits .313 in his first full season.

1918 Now an emerging star, Hornsby struggles along with major league baseball, which is affected by the intensifying World War. Hornsby is exempt from the draft, but eventually takes on a "war-essential" job in the shipyards at Wilmington, Delaware. He marries Sarah Martin on September 23.

1919 Hornsby makes his first visit to a dog track, beginning a long and notorious passion for gambling on horse and greyhound races.

1920 In the first season of the "lively ball era," Hornsby wins his first National League batting title with an average of .370. Rogers Hornsby Jr. is born in November.

1922 Hornsby is the first National League player to hit better than .400 in the twentieth century and sets a record with 250 hits. His efforts in the 1922 season comprise what is widely considered the best statistical season for a second baseman in history, hitting 42 home runs, scoring 141 runs, and driving in 152. He hit successfully in 135 of his 154 games, establishing a record shared with Chuck Klein that still stands.

1923 Aware of Hornsby's affair with Mary Jeannette Pennington Hine, Sarah Hornsby divorces her husband in June, receiving $25,000 and custody of Rogers Jr.

1924 Hornsby and Jeannette marry on February 28. Hornsby hits .424 to set the modern-day record for the highest single-season batting average. He finishes second in voting for Most Valuable Player to pitcher Dazzy Vance.

1925 Owner Sam Breadon names Hornsby player-manager of the St. Louis Cardinals on May 30. Hornsby's second son, William Pennington Hornsby, is born in St. Louis on June 2. Hornsby captures his second Triple Crown and is voted National League MVP. His .403 average secures him his sixth consecutive batting title.

1926 St. Louis wins its first National League pennant and first World Series, beating Babe Ruth and the New York Yankees in seven games. After a contract dispute in December, Breadon trades the championship player-manager to the New York Giants for infielder Frank Frisch and pitcher Jimmy Ring.

1927 After a successful season with the Giants, hitting well and filling in as manager for his friend John McGraw, Hornsby is traded again, this time to the Boston Braves.

1928 Braves owner Emil Fuchs names Hornsby player-manager early in the season, but after a dismal season on the field and in the accounting books, Fuchs is forced to trade his best player for financial relief. The Cubs give Fuchs five players and $200,000 for Hornsby, who had won his seventh batting title.

1929 Hornsby wins his second MVP award and second National League pennant. The Cubs lose the World Series to Connie Mack's Philadelphia Athletics in just five games. Hornsby has only five hits in twenty-one at-bats, striking out eight times.

1930 Suffering from bone spurs in his heels and, later, a broken ankle, Hornsby plays in only forty-two games. Cubs owner William Wrigley fires successful manager Joe McCarthy and announces that Hornsby will replace him in 1931.

1932 Chicago president William Veeck Sr. fires Hornsby on August 2. The Cubs reach the World Series and are swept by Joe McCarthy's Yankees.

1933 Sam Breadon and Branch Rickey offer Hornsby a chance to return to the Cardinals as a player under manager Gabby Street. After half a season with his old team, Hornsby switches leagues but not cities to become manager and part-time player for the last-place St. Louis Browns.

1937 After four disappointing seasons, new Browns owner Donald Barnes fires Hornsby, reputedly for repaying a debt with money won gambling on horse-races. Hornsby plays in his final major league game on July 20 against the Yankees. He finishes his career with a lifetime average of .358, second in history only to Ty Cobb.

1942 Hornsby, at the time manager of the Texas League's Fort Worth Cats, is elected to the National Baseball Hall of Fame. He is the sole inductee in 1942.

1945 Rogers and Jeannette Hornsby permanently separate.

1949 Rogers Hornsby Jr. dies in an airplane accident outside Savannah, Georgia, in December.

1950 Hornsby manages the Beaumont Roughnecks to their first Texas League title since before World War II.

1951 Hornsby manages the Seattle Rainiers to a Pacific Coast League pennant. In October, after fourteen years of minor league managerial jobs and part-time coaching gigs, Hornsby is hired by Bill Veeck Jr., new owner of the still-woeful St. Louis Browns, to manage in the major leagues again.

1952 Veeck fires Hornsby on June 10 after the Browns start the season 22–29. Cincinnati Reds owner Gabe Paul hires Hornsby to replace Luke Sewell as manager of his last place team.

1953 Paul fires Hornsby near the end of a disappointing season. Bernadette Harris, Hornsby's "good friend and secretary"—and reputed lover—jumps to her death from a Chicago apartment building owned by the ex-ballplayer. Hornsby publishes a memoir, edited by J. Roy Stockton, called *My Kind of Baseball*.

1957 Rogers Hornsby marries Majorie Porter on January 27 in Chicago. At the time, Hornsby is working in Mayor Richard Daley's administration, administering a youth baseball program.

1962 In the expansion team's first season, Hornsby takes a position as batting coach with the New York Mets, managed by his friend Casey Stengel. He publishes his second memoir, *My War with Baseball*, co-authored by Bill Surface.

1963 After complications from cataract surgery and a subsequent stroke, Hornsby dies of heart failure on January 5. He is buried at his family cemetery in Hornsby's Bend, Texas.

INTRODUCTION

It was an easy call at second base for umpire Bill Dinneen. "You're out," he shouted at Yankees slugger Babe Ruth, who was caught stealing to end Game 7 of the 1926 World Series. Rogers Hornsby, second baseman and field manager of the new major league champion St. Louis Cardinals, leapt joyfully after applying the tag and raced to the mound to hoist his friend Grover Cleveland Alexander off the ground. "Old Pete," as the veteran pitcher was known, had kept New York at bay for the game's last seven outs, including a soon-to-be famous strikeout of Tony Lazzeri, leading his team to the first championship in its history. The shouting pair were joined at the mound by catcher Bob O'Farrell, the National League's Most Valuable Player that season, who had made the decisive throw to Hornsby for the final out. The tag on Ruth that sealed the 3–2 victory, Hornsby would later say, was "my biggest thrill in all baseball."[1]

The afternoon celebration in Yankee Stadium with Alexander, O'Farrell, and the other Cardinals was Hornsby's chief display of team unity and achievement in a career that is memorable mostly for individual statistics and accomplishments. His playing experience in the major leagues began and ended with soft ground balls hit back to the pitcher, but most of his at-bats in between displayed much greater prowess with a bat. Standing at the back corner of the batter's box and stepping toward the plate upon the pitcher's release, Hornsby held his bat at its end and took level, powerful strokes. Over the course of more than twenty-one years, that swing achieved figures that remain some of the most awe-inspiring on record. While accumulating a lifetime batting average of .358, second best in the sport's history, Hornsby's single-season marks dwarfed those of most of his peers. He won batting titles in seven seasons, including 1924 when his final average was a daunting .424—a high-water mark for the modern era of baseball. As a winner of two Most Valuable Player awards as well as two National League Triple Crowns, Hornsby secured a permanent place among history's elite ballplayers. The "Rajah of Swat," as he was known, is widely regarded as the greatest hitter ever to swing his bat from the right side of the plate.

When Hornsby died in 1963, his obituary in the *Sporting News* concluded that his primary flaw had been holding "baseball in such high esteem that he could not tolerate those who did not."[2] Hornsby's passion for baseball was the key to a long and profitable life in the game, yet it was also his greatest handicap. Single-minded devotion to his daily task of striking leather with wood at times made him an uncommunicative and intolerant human being. As eager as his St. Louis teammates were to embrace him in October 1926, he would at other times be the most despised man in his clubhouse. On the occasions that he was granted the responsibility of managing teams, his quick and brutal criticisms often destroyed his players' will to win, which he at first tried desperately to build.

During his lifetime, Hornsby was known nearly as much for his personal conflicts as his on-field exploits. After his sudden rise from a skinny teenage stockyard employee, playing ball with men twice his age in Fort Worth, Texas, to the undisputed star of the National League, Hornsby became the most rootless of all his era's great players. At the peak of his career, Hornsby would be traded four times in four years. He served as manager for six major league teams and was fired twice by the same franchise. His skills were also coveted by shrewd baseball men like Branch Rickey and John McGraw, and he was once the centerpiece in the most expensive trade Organized Baseball had ever seen. However, Hornsby's stubborn refusal to be a "yes man," as he put it, cost him the trust of his owners and his players on almost every one of his teams. "Hornsby was as addicted to the truth as a drunk was to his bottle," a sportswriter once pithily wrote of him.[3] His unwavering commitment to speak his mind honestly on any topic, combined with his other notorious addiction—a strong compulsion to wager—turned the twisted course of his career several times.

Rogers Hornsby's greatest addiction, of course, was to the game of baseball, mostly at the expense of all other interests. Aside from his regular study of racing forms, Hornsby paid attention to little that happened away from ballparks, shunning even newspapers and motion pictures in the effort to keep his batting eyes strong. He famously slept up to twelve hours per night and ate thick steaks and pints of ice cream as often as possible, in the belief that these strict personal habits kept him fit. The result of the narrow course he followed is a life story that rarely leaves the diamond. His legacy, rather than in diaries, letters, and trunks full of personal artifacts, exists in strips of newsprint, in box scores, and in the recollections of those who watched his perfect swing drive baseballs into the dark corners of stadiums all around the United States. "It don't matter where I go or what happens, so long as I can play the full nine," he once said.[4] This book, therefore, focuses primarily on the time when Hornsby was actively participating in major league baseball, following the Rajah's circuitous path through a life that mattered most to him when he had a grip on a bat, a glint in his eye, and a good pitch on the way.

NOTES

1. Rogers Hornsby and Bill Surface, *My War with Baseball* (New York: Coward-McCann, 1962), 192.
2. *Sporting News*, January 19, 1963, 10.
3. *Boston Record-American*, January 8, 1963, 17.
4. Quoted in Tom Murray, *Sport Magazine's All-Time All Stars* (New York: Atheneum, 1977).

Rogers Hornsby, born in Texas in 1896, became the biggest star of the National League in the 1920s. *National Baseball Hall of Fame Library, Cooperstown, N.Y.*

STOCKYARDS AND SANDLOTS

Fort Worth, Texas, was a burgeoning urban area in the first decade of the twentieth century, when the state's ranchers began to supply a broader portion of the United States. The city's stockyards became the centralized finishing point for the beef industry and its population more than doubled between 1900 and 1910, climbing to nearly 75,000 inhabitants. Young Rogers Hornsby and his friends, traipsing from neighborhood to neighborhood outfitted in intricate uniforms sown by his mother, had no problem finding groups of like-minded kids to challenge to sandlot baseball games. Hopping trolleys to prearranged contests or wandering freshly finished roads in search of an empty lot and another listless team, Rogers and his comrades played baseball through the cloying summer heat and the dry, temperate winters, breaking only for school and the occasional football game.

That Rogers Hornsby was addicted to baseball from his earliest youth is not surprising. Fervid interest in the game was quickly spreading across the country. Since its origin in the northeastern states half a century before, baseball found participants and observers in almost every town with a population large enough to put two teams on a field. By the twentieth century, most American newspapers regularly reported the results of local games and accounts of the tremendously popular major leagues. Names like Willie Keeler, Honus Wagner, and Christy Mathewson were familiar to most schoolboys. Hornsby's oldest brother Everett, twelve years his senior, was already a professional baseball player, pitching spitballs for various minor league teams around Texas and the Midwest. Rogers' later claim that baseball was at the root of all his childhood memories is supported by the widespread passion for the game at the time and the professional interest within his own family. "I can't remember anything that happened before I had a baseball in my hand," he wrote in his first memoir.[1]

Before he picked up that baseball, Rogers Hornsby's life had begun in a setting much more similar to a dusty sandlot than a big city stadium. Located about 200 miles northwest of Austin, Runnels County, a flat stretch of land with little flora to speak of, is practically at the geographic center of Texas. In the late nineteenth century, the county's few inhabitants mostly operated small-scale ranches. In 1894, Ed Hornsby bought 640 acres of land from his brother Daniel. Ed moved with his wife Mary and their four children from the more populous Austin area to their new property near Winters, the tiny settlement center of Runnels County. In that home two years later, on April 27, 1896, the Hornsby family welcomed their fifth and final child, Rogers, who was born with blue eyes, fair hair, and features like his father.

Rogers Hornsby, named after his mother's family, was the great-grandson of an important figure in Texas history, a frontiersman who was among the first Anglo settlers in the region. Reuben Hornsby set out from Vicksburg, Mississippi, with his family and his slaves in 1830, seeking new plantation land. Working as a surveyor for Stephen F. Austin, Hornsby found amenable land and established a homestead at a sharp turn in the Colorado River valley, an area that was still a part of Mexico in the early 1830s. He named his settlement on the river Hornsby's Bend, and brought his family to live there permanently. Similar gatherings of pioneer families soon populated the region and together under Austin's supervision their settlements made up the "Little Colony." Reuben received his land as a grant from the Mexican government, but within a few years the area was part of the newly liberated Republic of Texas. A decade later, after Reuben Hornsby had gained local renown as a guide for the Texas Rangers and a stalwart defender of white settlements against attacks from uprooted Comanche, Texas joined the United States.

At his death in 1879, 86-year-old Reuben Hornsby was survived by only one of his ten children, but dozens of Hornsby offspring populated their eponymous little town in Travis County. In 1882, Reuben's grandson Ed married the teenaged Mary Dallas Rogers, who was herself a member of a large family that had settled an area near Hornsby's Bend called Rogers Hill. The couple lost their first child at birth but quickly had four more children in their first seven years of marriage. After Everett came two boys, Emory and William, and, in 1889, a daughter, Margaret. By the time their youngest brother was born, the other Hornsby children were occupied with helping their parents run the ranch and farm and were rarely, if ever, in school.

Ed Hornsby never had the chance to see his son Rogers guide a plow or throw a baseball. In mid-December 1898, 41-year-old Aaron Edward Hornsby died in the Runnels County cabin, leaving Mary with a toddler son and four other preadolescent children. After taking her husband's body to the cemetery at Hornsby's Bend, Mary and the children left their homestead and never returned, resettling with her parents at Rogers Hill. They would stay there about four years, long enough for young Rogers to pick up his first ball, but Mary Rogers Hornsby and her five children soon found a permanent home in a town growing as quickly as the six-year-old boy.

On January 10, 1901, an oil well drilled by a speculator at Spindletop, near Beaumont, spurted a burst of crude petroleum that literally changed the course of Texas history. It was the first discovery of oil in the state, which until that time had been only a site of investigative drilling. The discovery created a new local industry and a massive influx of cash and jobs. As money poured in with oil prospectors, Texas grew rapidly, and cities like Dallas, Fort Worth, Houston, and Austin became centers of trade. Fort Worth, formerly a dispatch point for cattle headed to Chicago and other cities with larger stockyards, suddenly had the resources and the demand to become a major meatpacking city unto itself.

Two giant meat companies, Swift and Armour, arrived in Fort Worth only months before the Hornsby family. By early 1903, when Mary and her children were established in a small but new house they rented across a creek from the stockyards, thousands of Texans had secured jobs with one of the two big meatpacking companies. At that time, more of Fort Worth's approximately 25,000 residents were employed as "packers" than in all other occupations combined, and most of those other jobs were in services peripheral to the financial boom, such as hotels, merchant shops, saloons, and whorehouses.[2] Over the next several years, the three older Hornsby brothers—the youngest of whom, William, was still only fifteen when he went to work full-time—supported their mother and siblings by putting in long hours at the stockyard complex in North Fort Worth.

His brothers' triple income allowed Rogers time to attend school in the newly minted Fort Worth public education system. It also afforded him the leisure to play, practice, and watch baseball whenever he wasn't in class. He and his fellow youth had been playing organized games for a few years even before Rogers started attending the packers' games. Mary Hornsby had sewn uniforms for the boys out of blue flannel, and her son wore his religiously, not only as a member of two different neighborhood teams, but also around his own yard, so proud was he of the feeling of "importance" that a sharp uniform gave him. Baseball played in a uniform was closer to the proper form of the game that the obsessed youth admired; Rogers was desperate to join the adult games as early as possible.

In an interview after his early success in the major leagues, Hornsby said that even "before I was able to lisp my letters, I guess, I had decided to adopt the game as a profession."[3] His first work, however, could only be described as baseball-related in that the people he worked with were interested in and played baseball themselves. At 10, the Swift Company hired him as an occasional messenger, sending him around the stockyards or around town on small errands. He soon earned a more regular position as assistant to J. P. Elder, the superintendent of Swift and Company in Fort Worth. Elder was kind to Rogers and the boy responded to the father figure with a quick and steady loyalty. His allegiance to his boss was so evident that coworkers nicknamed Hornsby "Dick" because he "resembled a sleuth trailing [Elder] from one end of the plant to another."[4]

The quiet and respectful young employee was an irrepressible conversationalist if the subject of baseball came up, and his passion led to an invitation to join a team of Swift employees as a batboy of sorts, tending to the team's equipment in exchange for cast-off balls or bats or the occasional opportunity to fill in at any position in the later innings of a game. When Hornsby moved on to a job with the railroad the summer following his work with Elder, he discovered that his full-time schedule prevented him from participating in baseball games. Informed by Mary Hornsby of his former employee's distress, Elder conferred with Rogers' new boss and had the schedule amended.

In 1909, Hornsby was a ninth-grader at Fort Worth's North Side High School. No records of his academic performance remain, nor were statistics of his athletic feats consistently kept. As a high school baseball player, he was remembered as a standout pitcher; teammates thought of him as "a coming Mathewson." His focus on pitching left him without a specialty in the field, and on days that he didn't take the mound, Rogers "played every position on that school team," even catcher.[5]

In athletic talent, Hornsby did not stand out. Aside from his unimposing physical stature—he was about five-feet eleven-inches tall and weighed just 135 pounds at the end of high school—he also failed to distinguish himself as his school's best athlete. Although he was the team's best pitcher and ran in the football team's backfield, he was not alone in athletic achievement among his friends. Rogers was one of six students at North Side High of approximately his age who went on to have prolific professional careers in various sports. All six came from the tough stockyard district, "that part of the city that held terror for the corduroy and velvet adorned youth."[6]

His fellow running back, Bo McMillan, was a much bigger celebrity than Hornsby in their school days. McMillan went on to Centre College and became an All-American as a "Praying Colonel." He had a successful professional football career as well and became the head coach at Geneva College in Beaver Falls, Pennsylvania. Three other teammates also played football at Centre College: Bill James and Matt Bell had long coaching careers afterward at the University of Texas and Texas Christian University, respectively, while Sully Montgomery followed his college football days as a nationally recognized professional boxer. Pete Donohue, who entered North Side around the time Hornsby left the school, became a better pitcher than Hornsby ever was. Donohue pitched for the Texas Christian baseball team and signed with the Cincinnati Reds. He earned a spot in the team's rotation in the middle of the 1921 season and, by the time he retired eleven seasons later, had accumulated 134 wins and a 3.87 career earned run average.[7]

Unlike the perpetual schedule of sandlot games, the high school baseball season was finite and gave way to the other quickly growing Texas sports passion—football. Although Rogers also enjoyed football, once his mates started playing it as often as baseball, his attention turned increasingly toward the teams on which his brothers and coworkers played. At fifteen, he dropped out of high school and went back to work for Elder. At the same time, the Swift team promoted him from batboy to the regular third baseman. He was proud to play with the men, although his spot in the lineup was more a testament to his persistence than to his talent. The men let him participate in the city league "not because I was good," he later acknowledged, "but because I loved to play so much that they couldn't get rid of me."[8]

The experience undoubtedly helped Hornsby prepare for his professional career. Just before his eighteenth birthday in 1914, Hornsby had a tryout with the Dallas Steers of the Texas League, at the time a respected Class B league.[9] His brother Everett, deep into a journeyman's minor league career and now pitching spitballs for Dallas, arranged for the audition. His experience playing against the men in the Forth Worth city league obviously gave the younger Hornsby the confidence he needed to try out against experienced professionals. His pluck and his rigorously practiced fielding skills earned him a spot with the team and a small contract.

He didn't last long. In two weeks with the team, the manager never put Rogers in a game and he did little more than catch his brother's warm-up pitches. He was released without warning, although the small sum he was paid confirmed his belief that he could make money playing ball. Opportunities were scarce for the skinny teenager around home. After a few more weeks with the railroad company, a chance to earn a few more dollars on the diamond presented itself and proved that earning glory in the game was not Hornsby's highest priority. The basic pay agreement with his new team had one important caveat: Rogers would have to play in drag.

The Boston Bloomer Girls were touring the southwest playing exhibitions and, short a few players, advertised for replacements. Hornsby and a friend sought out the promoter, Logan Galbreath, and asked if they might fill a pair of outfield spots. Galbreath needed players, but insisted that they be *female* players. The three men reached a compromise. Donning skirts and wigs, Rogers and his friend played in most of the team's Dallas-area games. They were paid only seventy-eight cents apiece for their contributions, and their vaudeville act was never discovered by the crowds that came to watch the games. Years later Hornsby would repeat the story several times, alternately amused and embarrassed by his younger self, but the detail that he never revealed was the quality of his performance in those games. Whether due to his respect for his female teammates, his modesty, or perhaps his humility at unremarkable achievement against opponents of the "weaker" sex, Rogers' statistics as a cross-dressing outfielder are not available.

The relationship between Rogers and his mother Mary was devoted and mutually supportive, particularly in the years after his brothers had moved from the family house. His mother and his sister Margaret relied on his earnings once he began to work full-time, but his dream to follow his oldest brother into professional baseball meant that he would have to give up his regular employment and likely play for a fraction of what he might earn in the stockyards. Mary Hornsby had always encouraged her youngest son's singular interest in the sport to a degree beyond mere motherly indulgence, so when Rogers declared that he wanted to travel to a few towns where he might get tryouts for minor league teams, she gave her blessing. He assured her that he'd return home the day his season ended and guaranteed that he would work hard enough at baseball to earn at least as much money as he would as a packer.

As the early summer heat was building, Hornsby informed Elder of his plans and arranged to return to his place on Swift's floor in the fall. He took a bus north to Oklahoma and almost immediately caught on with a team in Hugo that played in the Texas-Oklahoma League, a newly established Class D league. His contract paid about $75 per month, much better than the $2 per week he had earned in the semipro city league. Rogers quickly gave up hope of becoming a pitcher like his brother, claiming to love the game too much to limit himself to pitching. His versatility in the field earned the respect of his manager, who installed him as Hugo's starting shortstop but batted him near the bottom of the line-up. Hornsby must have felt doomed to a career of short engagements when, just as he was fielding well and finally growing accustomed to hitting against professionals, the Hugo team folded for financial reasons six weeks into the season.

However, Hugo's dismantling was actually a fortuitous turn for Hornsby. The organization, too far in debt to continue to field a team but also beholden to its players' contracts, sold or gave away players to various other minor league teams around the South. Hornsby had made a favorable impression on Hugo's owners and their enthusiasm for him convinced a team in Denison, Texas, to purchase his meager contract for $125.

The Denison Railroaders played in the Western Association, a better recognized and better organized Class D league. Although there was more than half a season remaining at the time he joined the team, the eighteen-year-old Hornsby did not fit right into the lineup. He resumed his "play me where you need me" philosophy and earned manager Babe Peebles's respect with his work ethic if not with his performance. In 1914, his batting average was only .232 and he made 45 errors over 113 games. It was not his numbers but the hours that the young student of baseball devoted to improving them that warranted his invitation to return to the club for the following season.

After an off-season living in his mother's house and working at the Swift plant, Rogers headed back to Denison in March for spring training, which consisted of practices interspersed with exhibitions against major league clubs looking for preseason tune-ups before returning north to begin their seasons. Hornsby won himself a regular role that spring; judged as the best glove on the team, he took over as the starting shortstop and, even though the result was a whopping 58 errors in his 119 games, he stayed at the position as long as he was with the team. He was also playing well enough to attract the attention of opposing coaches and players.

The second half of the St. Louis Cardinals split squad was one of the major league outfits that stopped in Denison for a training series. That spring, the team was managed by the organization's chief scout, Bob Connery, who evaluated the Cardinals young talent during training camp and sought out other promising youths during the rest of the year. In three exhibitions that the Cardinals handled easily, Connery clearly saw enough potential in his opponent's ranks to schedule a personal return to Denison later that season. Although Hornsby did not know it, he had played his way onto Bob Connery's scouting list.

Toward the end of the Western Association season, Connery reappeared in Denison to check up on the shortstop who had impressed him five months earlier. Although he saw a considerably improved hitter—standing away from the plate and holding his bat at the very end, Hornsby hit .277 in a league with only a handful of .300 hitters—Connery remained primarily interested in

Hornsby's fielding. Despite his numerous errors, the scout thought Hornsby had "great hands" and an exceptional arm. Intent on seeing him at his best, Connery even bought the young man a new glove and cleats out of his own pocket.[10]

After watching a few games and running Hornsby through a few drills, Connery met with Railroaders' owner Roy Finley. As the representative of St. Louis's National League franchise, he arranged the purchase of Hornsby's contract—still only $75 a month—for $500. Finley met Rogers in the Denison clubhouse and told him the good news: the Cardinals had asked Hornsby to meet the team for a series against the Cincinnati Reds and to play out the final month of their season as a part-time infielder.

Hornsby rushed to join his new ballclub. On September 2, 1915, he sent his mother an excited telegram, bought a secondhand jacket, and packed his small carpetbag. The next day, with just three dollars in his billfold, he boarded a train bound for Cincinnati and the National League.

NOTES

1. Rogers Hornsby, *My Kind of Baseball*, ed. J. Roy Stockton (New York: David McKay, 1953), 29.

2. Charles Alexander, *Rogers Hornsby* (New York: Henry Holt, 1995), 14.

3. "Hornsby from Sand Lots Raises Lots of Dust," *Sporting News*, May 1917.

4. Arthur Mann, "New York's New Babe Ruth: Rogers Hornsby, The Story of His Life," *New York Evening World*, January 11, 1927.

5. "Hornsby from Sand Lots Raises Lots of Dust."

6. "Six Stars Once Boyhood Chums," *New York Sun*, February 9, 1928.

7. Ibid.

8. Hornsby, *My Kind of Baseball*, 33.

9. The National Association of Professional Baseball Leagues, created in 1902 and essentially the governing body of the disorganized institution colloquially known as Organized Baseball, had four classifications for the minor leagues in 1914: A, B, C, and D, with A the highest and D the lowest.

10. Alexander, *Rogers Hornsby*, 20.

GROWING INTO THE NATIONAL LEAGUE

When Miller Huggins, the manager of the Cardinals, first saw his new utility player, he was skeptical about the kid's future. "Pale and pimpled" with close-cropped hair, unable to fill out his shirt, and "full of a certain sort of nervous energy," the 19-year-old recruit was physically unimposing.[1] Once Huggins reviewed Hornsby's Denison statistics, he was also dismayed that Connery had spent $500 of the organization's funds for a weak-hitting, error-prone shortstop who weighed less than 140 pounds. Hornsby got off a train in Cincinnati the morning of September 3, 1915 and made his way to Crosley Field, home of the Reds. His manager shook his hand and said little in greeting, then watched as the new Cardinal took batting practice. Unimpressed, Huggins decided to let Hornsby get a feel for the major leagues before using him in a game.

Rogers Hornsby first saw the city of St. Louis on September 6, when the Cardinals returned to their home stadium, Robison Field, for a long, season-ending homestand. After winning three of four against the Chicago Cubs they dropped both games of a double-header to the Reds on September 9. With a record of 65–69, it was clear that the Cardinals had no chance of pennant contention. Huggins had no choice but to try out the young players Connery and the other team scouts were sending to St. Louis in the hope of building a winning franchise for the future. Hornsby was the latest in a series of teenagers culled from the lower levels of the minor leagues for Huggins to evaluate. So, in the sixth inning on September 10, the manager called down the bench to his young charge and sent Hornsby out to pinch hit against the Reds' rookie pitcher Charles "King" Lear.

Hornsby (left) shaking hands with his first major league manager, Miller Huggins, before the 1926 World Series between the Cardinals and the New York Yankees. *National Baseball Hall of Fame Library, Cooperstown, N.Y.*

Asked a few years later if he was nervous in his first plate appearance, Hornsby replied, "Naw, why should I be nervous? The other birds was hittin' him."[2] Hornsby's memory was not entirely accurate, for Lear held the Cardinals to just a single run in his complete game victory. Moreover, fraught with nervousness or not, Hornsby's two at-bats yielded only two groundball outs. Huggins left the initiated youth on the bench for another few days after that first appearance, but on September 13, he inserted Hornsby into the starting lineup at shortstop against Brooklyn. Rogers would be turning double plays with his manager, who was finishing his playing career at second base that season. His first start was uneventful: no errors but also no hits in a loss.

Rogers' first major league hit came the next day, a single against a well-regarded pitcher named Rube Marquand. In batting practice, Huggins was critical of Hornsby's long swing that was the result of his stance at the back of the batter's box and his grip at the very end of the bat. Hornsby was too small for his swing, Huggins said. Using his own batting style as an example, he had the light young man choke up 6 inches on his bat and move closer to the plate. Hornsby's contact increased, and he hit .246 when Huggins kept him as the starting shortstop over the final fifteen games.

The shorter, quicker swing was more effective, but it failed to impress many people in St. Louis. The fact that he made an error every other game likewise did little for his reputation. Asked about Hornsby's future with the Cardinals, Huggins was blunt about his plans for the next season: he liked Hornsby's attitude and willingness to learn, "but he's a bit awkward up there at the plate. Looks like he's too young and too light. Maybe with a couple of years in the minors he'll develop, but I'm trying to get Roy Corhan from the Pacific Coast League, and he'll be my shortstopper for 1916."[3]

Bob Connery also thought Roy Corhan was a prime prospect, but the friendship he'd developed with his young recruit from the Western Association led him to approach Huggins on Hornsby's behalf. "The kid loves to play ball. He doesn't drink or smoke. He'll make it," the scout assured the manager. He added, by way of a guarantee, "and if he doesn't, I'll pay that five hundred."[4] Connery's comments may be apocryphal, but it is clear that neither Huggins nor any other St. Louis official would have asked him to repay Hornsby's purchase price by the time the rookie had played a full season.

Even considering his friend's exhortations, the manager wasn't certain he would give Hornsby a chance at a full major league season—at least not in 1916. After a one-game trip to Chicago to finish their season and a six-game postseason "City Series" against the St. Louis Browns, Huggins met with each player to discuss their performance and offer good wishes for the off-season ahead. When Hornsby came into the manager's office at Robison Field, Huggins thanked him for his hustle and his dedication to improving himself. He was welcome to join the team for training the next spring, but given his errors and his light swing, it was likely they were "going to have to farm you out for next year," Huggins told his young charge.[5] This was before the organization of formal "farm systems" for major league franchises, but Huggins meant that Hornsby would probably need some more time playing in the farm towns of the minor leagues. Hornsby's interpretation was likely the most fortuitous and famous misunderstanding of his life.

It became a story repeated in newspaper columns, in books, and during radio broadcasts for the rest of his career. The 18-year-old Hornsby, heeding his manager's "advice," had his mother arrange for him to spend the fall and winter working on her brother-in-law's dairy farm in Lockhart, Texas. Though it was not exactly the prescription Huggins had given, Hornsby established a regimen that transformed his gangly figure into the mature body of a professional athlete. Rising each day at five A.M. and retiring in the evening by eight, he found enough work, food, and sleep to put at least 20 pounds onto his 5-feet 11-inch frame. He ate thick steaks frequently and drank milk in quantities almost impossible anywhere but on a dairy farm; their effects convinced him to keep beef and milk as the main staples of his diet throughout his life.

Late in February 1916, the Cardinals convened in Hot Wells, Texas at the Terrell Hotel for their annual spring camp. Hornsby shocked everyone when he got off the train weighing about 165 pounds. A contract had been sent to him at his mother's house in Fort Worth that promised to pay $2,000 for the season if he made the team's final roster. After Connery and Huggins saw the now-strapping youth drive balls all over Hot Wells, the contract seemed secure. Hornsby was naturally impetuous, but with his confidence bolstered further by his strength, he had reversed his manager's instructions and returned to standing away from the plate and swinging from the end of the bat. The Cardinals had paid an astounding $15,000 to San Francisco to get Corhan, so he and not Hornsby would necessarily be the team's shortstop, but the coaches felt certain that the Texan and his bat would have a role on the team.

While the U.S. Army pursued Pancho Villa throughout Mexico and southwest Texas, the Cardinals finished training and played a final string of exhibition games that led them home to St. Louis for an annual preseason series against the city's American League entry, the Browns. The 1916 season figured to be an improvement for each organization, at least in regard to finances, because the dissolution of the Federal League, and with it the St. Louis Terriers, meant that the city's fans would have only two outlets for their major league baseball interest—and for their ticket money.[6]

The establishment of the Federal League in 1913 had sent tremors through the establishment of Organized Baseball. The meteoric rise of national interest in professional baseball had brought profit and celebrity to major league owners and players alike, and the Federal League, although its existence was brief, was the only legitimate competition ever posed against the two traditional major leagues. In 1913, the league began play as nothing more than a Class C-level minor league with a broader geographical spread than most; teams were located in Chicago, Cleveland, Covington, Kentucky, Indianapolis, Kansas City, Pittsburgh, and St. Louis. In 1914, however, with a huge infusion of money and a charismatic league president named Jim Gilmore, the Feds, as they were known, announced their intention to compete with the National and American Leagues as a "major" league, adding franchises in Baltimore, Brooklyn, and Buffalo.

Few established stars of the time jumped leagues—Mordecai "Three Finger" Brown and Joe Tinker were the most famous—but the wildly popular Cy Young did agree to manage the Cleveland team. Another of the great pitchers of the era, Washington Senator Walter Johnson, also agreed to a contract to pitch for the Chicago Whales in 1915, until Washington owner Clark Griffith convinced the other American League owners to help pay for a salary increase to keep the "Big Train" in Washington for "the good of the league." There were similar threats, but, for the most part, the damage to the established leagues came from the defection of scores of players with average abilities and salaries, the players who supported the stars and kept the standard of play acceptable for major league fans.

In St. Louis, the damage was palpable. Neither the Cardinals nor the Browns had enjoyed the benefit of a bona fide star player; without drawing cards, attendance at their respective venues fluctuated with their on-field success and the fans' whimsy, although in recent seasons the Cardinals had fared far worse. The greatest damage had come in 1915, when both the Cardinals at Robison Field and the Browns at Sportsman's Park six blocks up the road notably failed to draw as many paying fans as the Federal League's pennant-chasing St. Louis Terriers.[7] Several St. Louis major leaguers had defected to the Terriers and other Federal teams as well. The combination of Cardinals deteriorating financial situation and their absolute dearth of quality players is very likely the sole reason that Rogers Hornsby was ever signed to the major league team in the first place. Players from the lower minor leagues were cheap and plentiful; the chance that Connery would find a diamond in the rough was all the franchise could afford.

The Federal League itself, despite winning skirmishes in cities like St. Louis, was unable to afford its continued war with Organized Baseball once battles started taking place in courtrooms across the country. Kenesaw Mountain Landis, a well-known federal judge, a dedicated legal foe of monopolies, and a serious follower of baseball, had surprisingly chosen to rule against the Federal

League's antitrust action versus Organized Baseball; the continued litigation in the aftermath of his ruling proved too expensive to continue, even with the backing of a number of millionaires. The Feds acquiesced and chose to disband. The two sides did reach a resolution that compensated Federal League owners for the costs of dismantling their franchises and also allowed a few of those owners the opportunity to buy major league organizations. Philip Ball, the owner of the Terriers, purchased the Browns and Sportsman's Park with them. The investors in the Baltimore Federal League franchise made a proposal to purchase the Cardinals and move the franchise to Maryland, but after extended negotiations in the Federal League settlement, owner Helene Robison Britton retained ownership and the team stayed on at Robison Field.

The 1916 season would be St. Louis's twenty-fifth in the National League, and it promised to be a season as dismal as most of the others had been. A perennial "second-division" team—the traditional term for teams in the second half of the standings—the Cardinals had been losing games and losing money under the ownership of Mrs. Britton and her husband, team president Schuyler Britton, since she inherited the team from her father and uncle in 1911. The folding of the Terriers meant a potential boost in paying fans, but that potential was undermined by the financial predicament of a team that could not afford to stock its clubhouse with quality players or even to sign former Terriers, many of whom followed Phil Ball up the road to the Browns.

The team needed a star. Though Hornsby's spring performance demonstrated a severe improvement over his first games as a Cardinal, neither the Brittons nor Miller Huggins nor even Bob Connery had any hope that he could become their team's premier attraction. Hornsby himself could not have anticipated the fantastic leap to stardom he was about to make. By the end of 1916, however, the 20-year-old Texan had earned significant national attention. Within a few seasons, he would be a true major league celebrity and the most famous Cardinal in his team's history.

The fans who turned out to watch the exhibitions between the Browns and Cardinals over the week of April 4–10, 1916 came to watch another player who had made his major league debut the previous season. The Browns' George Sisler, a year past his graduation from the University of Michigan and an acrimonious battle over which major league team had claim to him, was the city's sensation that spring, having both pitched and hit with assurance during his first professional campaign. Branch Rickey, the Browns' manager in 1915, was himself a Michigan graduate and had run the college's team and coached Sisler there before moving to St. Louis. Happy to have the talented young man, Rickey proclaimed Sisler a future star—"the equal of Ty Cobb," even—and praised the pitcher–first baseman's dedication to the training drills Rickey had developed.[8]

But when Phil Ball bought the Browns, he pulled Rickey from the dugout in favor of Fielder Jones and made him the only full-time business manager, much to the deposed field captain's dismay. The Browns were the city's superior team in that opening series and throughout the upcoming season, thanks in part to Sisler's roundly excellent play, and St. Louisans credited Rickey for much of the achievment, cementing his reputation as a brilliant baseball mind.

Miller Huggins was a keen baseball mind himself, though of a more traditional persuasion than the experimenting Rickey. He mocked the cross-town "genius" and his concocted drills, such as sliding practice taken in sandpits, as well as the Browns' complex defensive schemes. Huggins, who had a law degree like Rickey, sparked a public feud between the two men when he said managing was about leadership and decision making, not theorizing.[9]

The best decision Huggins made in 1916 was one of simple necessity more than prescience. Roy Corhan injured his shoulder on the route north to St. Louis, and though Huggins reluctantly played Artie Butler at short through the rest of the spring schedule, he decided to go with the "milk-fed" Hornsby for the preseason City Series. Satisfied that Hornsby would hit at least as well as Butler, Huggins slotted the young utility player into the starting lineup—hitting sixth and playing shortstop—on April 12 against the Pittsburgh Pirates. It would be the first of eleven consecutive Opening Day starts that Hornsby would make for the Cardinals.

Playing opposite his boyhood idol Honus Wagner—still an imposing batsman and strong fielder at 42 years old—Hornsby was the hero of St. Louis's 2–1 victory. The National League's elder statesman started his twentieth season by going 3-for-3 for Pittsburgh, but its future star had 2 hits in his 3 at-bats and knocked in both Cardinals runs. Though his throwing error led to the Pirates' only run, Hornsby's bunt on a squeeze play in the bottom of the ninth allowed Bruno Betzel to make the winning tally.

His visibly improved batting skills, his enhanced physical stature, and his place in the lineup excited Hornsby and earned respect from some teammates who had been unconvinced of the young man's abilities. They had nicknamed him "Pep" while in Hot Wells because of his vigor during training but had treated him much like the men in the Fort Worth city league had: as an overly enthusiastic young man who loved playing and talking about baseball. The fact that he would hit as well as any Cardinal during the 1916 season, however, convinced them that his enthusiasm had produced positive results. "The other fellows are always willing to help a youngster along if you aren't too fresh," he told *Sporting News* writer Dick Collins. "It takes pluck and push to get ahead, but one doesn't have to trample on other people to make good in baseball."[10]

The Cardinals record did not mirror Hornsby's personal improvement. Wins did not come easily for Huggins' squad that season. Sportswriters around the country who predicted a woeful season for the Redbirds took little pride in seeing their projections hold true, for the team's general ineptitude was clear even to casual observers. In a typical article assessing the Cardinals, the *New York Times* summed up their abilities by claiming that Brooklyn manager Wilbert Robinson could "blindfold his rawest recruits, and welding them into a team . . . send them out to everlastingly extinguish the St. Looey outfit."[11] Losing far more frequently than they had in 1915, that outfit finished seventh in the National League with a record of 60–93.

Hornsby and a few other players did give their manager reason to look ahead to the next season. Corhan returned to action in May and proved that he was ready for major league play, as he hit adequately and played a consistent shortstop. Hornsby's hot bat had earned him Huggins's respect and a permanent place in the line-up by the time Corhan was healthy, but in order to play both young men at the same time, the manager chose to move Pep to third base. The defensive move took advantage of Hornsby's quick release of the baseball and also reduced the opportunities for his occasionally wild arm to miss its target. Huggins actually freely moved Hornsby around the infield that season, though the bulk of his time was spent at third. He took his turn at second base and occasionally at first, a position where a few newspapermen thought he was "destined to be at his best."[12]

It did not take long for observers around the league to notice Hornsby's capacity to hit hard line drives to all fields. Brooklyn's Robinson praised his batting form and the power it produced, though Hornsby's first home run as a Cardinal—against Robinson's team on May 14 in St. Louis—was no awe-inspiring feat. A spinning blooper to shallow left, the ball had landed just inside the foul line and bounced toward the grandstand, skipping off the rail and into the stands. By the rules of the day, any fair ball that subsequently bounced out of play earned the batter a round trip. The first five-hit game of his career came in a victory in Cincinnati on June 28 and included a more decisive home run. His .301 average on July 6 put him among the league leaders, as did his 6 home runs.

While playing veterans acknowledged the young man's skills, the newspapers were ready to declare Hornsby a future star. The *Sporting News* was the most respected baseball-oriented publication in the country. Founded in 1886 by brothers Alfred and Charles Spink and based in St. Louis, the paper was run by J. G. Taylor Spink, Charles' son, and had a national distribution and an editorial policy to cover baseball in all major league cities, not just St. Louis. The inevitable bias of proximity aside, Spink and his editors cited Hornsby as the National League's "best youngster," calling him a "star of the first water" whose talent demanded that the public "sit up and take notice."[13] The *St. Louis Post-Dispatch* ran a feature at mid-season that detailed his jump from the small Western Association to the top of the National League's offensive leaderboards. He was "the prize of the 1916 youngsters" the major Midwestern paper declared, and had "already created [a] stir" by, among other things, "hitting the hardest ball in the circuit."[14]

After national publications and opposing players and managers declared their admiration of Hornsby's skills, other franchises inevitably began approaching the Cardinals owners with trade offers for Hornsby. The Brittons listened to Chicago Cubs owner Charles Weegham's offer to buy Hornsby outright and Brooklyn's proposed deal involving multiple players such as shortstop Ollie O'Mara and outfielder Casey Stengel. Helene and Schuyler Britton were facing a personal financial crisis that had begun to impinge on their operation of the team and to dismantle their marriage; despite their problems, however, the owner and team president resisted all offers for the Cardinal.[15]

Any attempt to improve the club by trading Hornsby would have come far too late in 1916. By the end of the season, he was the only Cardinal hitting with any consistency. Huggins moved him to the cleanup spot and though he did not hit a home run in the second half of the season, his run production increased with his batting average. On September 14, the formerly unknown Texan was close to becoming the National League's batting champion. Hitting at a .320 rate, he was a mere .002 behind league leader Hal Chase of Cincinnati. Chase finished the season strong while the Reds did not, and Hornsby slumped slightly as the Cardinals slumped horribly. The result would put Chase well ahead of Hornsby for the batting title, but their teams, after St. Louis lost their final fourteen games, settled into a comfortable last place tie.

Hornsby's numbers for the season were remarkable for a player whose manager had thought belonged in the minor leagues a year before. His .313 batting average was fourth best in the league (and only .003 points away from second), while his 6 home runs, 36 runs scored and 60 runs batted in led his team and kept pace with the league's best. He had even performed better than the vaunted Sisler, who had hit .305 up the street for the Browns. Most importantly to the avid ballplayer, his success and the modest amount of fame that came with it meant that Hornsby would certainly have a place on the roster again the next year.

Hornsby found his off-season much more peaceful than most other people involved in St. Louis baseball would. He returned home to his mother's house and took a job on the floor of the Swift plant. He visited a young woman he'd met in Denison named Sarah Martin, enjoyed the company of his mother and sister, worked hard at his job and at staying in condition, and talked to anyone who asked about life in the major leagues.

Meanwhile, the Cardinals organization was in turmoil. The personal tension between the Brittons escalated to a full-scale divorce trial, in which Miller Huggins, as their primary employee, was forced to testify. After the settlement, with most of the Cardinals away from St. Louis with their families and Huggins back at his off-season home in Cincinnati, Helene Robison Britton announced that her team was up for sale.

Financial difficulties were not a new phenomenon in the organization, but with American involvement in the First World War dampening the economy in St. Louis and small hope of immediate improvement, Mrs. Britton had little interest in keeping the team in her broken family. Her father and uncle had led a group of investors that, in 1899, had purchased the St. Louis Browns, who had become part of the National League seven years before. Frank and Stanley Robison decided that the team needed a facelift: they built a new facility (Robison Field), scrapped the brown-trimmed uniforms, and renamed their squad the Perfectos. The bright, eye-catching red lines on the new uniforms quickly inspired a more accurate nickname that focused less attention on the team's less than perfect play. As the twentieth century began, the city's National League team became known as the Cardinals and a new team in the nascent American League resumed use of the name St. Louis Browns.

When both Robison brothers died early in the 1910s, they bequeathed their majority share in the Cardinals to Frank's daughter Helene, who was the first female owner in major league history. Her decision to sell the team in 1917 raised the possibility that the team would not just leave the family, but the city as well. Mrs. Britton's asking price for her franchise was $350,000, though she openly stated that she would be willing to accept the money in installments. Her expectation, it seems, was that Miller Huggins would find the proposal attractive enough to purchase the organization to run himself. The Cardinals manager did not have the money to buy the team alone, and the investors he connected with were a pair of yeast magnates from Cincinnati, brothers named Fleischmann. The small group offered $75,000 as a down payment, but as soon as they did so rumors arose that if Huggins and the Fleischmanns bought the franchise, they would move it to their hometown.

The Cardinals team attorney James Jones gambled that the city would resist the team's relocation. St. Louis, a city of over 700,000 at the time, made a surprising rally around their hapless Cardinals. The city had given barely a murmur when the team was almost moved to Baltimore the year before and had supported the Browns with much more vigor in 1916. But much like when her father and uncle had bought the team at the head of a group of local businessmen, this transition of ownership came with widespread support. Jones made a public offering of stock, and after more than 1,500 people subsequently invested, he was able to offer an initial payment of $50,000 to Mrs. Britton. She was devoted to her friend Huggins but also to her family's legacy in St. Louis. She accepted the offer from Jones' group.

The sale was confirmed in February 1917, and Jones immediately set out to solidify the organization. A fan of baseball but not an expert, he consulted a group of St. Louis sportswriters and editors to ask whom they felt would make a team president best-suited to lead the Cardinals back to success. Their unanimous reply was Branch Rickey.

Rickey and Phil Ball had established a peaceful, efficient working relationship in the Browns' front office. Ball, a cantankerous, self-made millionaire, was always suspicious of the erudite general manager, however. He respected Rickey's canny baseball strategy but dismissed his moralistic worldview, derisively calling the Methodist Rickey "the goddamned prohibitionist."[16] Anxious at the opportunity to become a team president, Rickey approached the Browns' owner for permission to take the job Jones had offered. Ball hastily agreed, but later attempted to block Rickey's move after American League president Ban Johnson convinced him that losing the innovative Rickey would be against the best interests of the Browns and the league itself. By the end of March, Jones and Ball settled their dispute over Rickey—who by that point had been working for the Cardinals for over a month—and Rickey signed a contract with the Cardinals that paid the new president $15,000 a year.

While the two organizations fought over Rickey's contractual obligations, Rickey was resolving a contract negotiation with the young star of his team. Hornsby, a willing player who had never bothered to argue his payment terms before and whose mother had to sign all his contracts until he turned 21, arrived at spring training demanding twice the salary he had earned the year before. He knew he was the key piece to Rickey's puzzle of young players and sought to take advantage of it. He did not ask for a salary similar to established stars like Ty Cobb and Tris Speaker, who earned between $15,000 and $20,000, but even his modest demands were denied. The team was strapped for cash—investors still owed Helene Britton nearly $200,000—and Rickey simply could not agree to pay Hornsby $8,000 over two seasons. Both sides ended dissatisfied by the discussions, but finally agreed to a single season contract for $3,000.

The team trained for the third straight year at Hot Wells, Texas, and boarded at the undignified Terrell Hotel. This was another financial imperative forced upon Rickey, who had trained the Browns in St. Petersburg, Florida, and believed warmer weather and comfortable accommodations benefited rusty players reacclimating their bodies to the game. A further distraction was part of the training agenda in 1917: military drills for the players under the instruction of Army recruiters. With President Woodrow Wilson's stance of neutrality in the

European war eroding and the deployment of American troops imminent, major league owners agreed that their players should prepare for both baseball and military service. This patriotic distraction aside, Huggins and Hornsby both enjoyed training in Texas, and the team had a promising training season.

Roy Corhan had played his way back to the Pacific Coast League over the latter half of the previous season and Rickey and Huggins chose not to offer Artie Butler a new contract, so Hornsby took over as shortstop on a team that barely resembled 1916's pathetic outfit. Hornsby, at his new position, and outfielders Jack Smith and Tommy Long were the only everyday players that kept their spots in the starting lineup. The change was positive. The 1917 Cardinals won twenty-two more games than they did the year before, and Hornsby stood out offensively on a team that, while never imposing, could score runs consistently. Still called "Pep" by teammates, the shortstop was a part of 82 double plays, most in the league at his position, though he still left Huggins shaking his head at his 52 errors.

If Hornsby's bat took the National League by surprise in his first full season, the opposition's awareness in the new season did little to help them stop it. Not only did his average improve to .327, second to Cincinnati's Edd Rousch, he scored 86 runs and knocked in 66, and led the league with 17 triples. Perhaps more remarkable for such a young player was his discipline at the plate. He drew 45 walks that season against an astonishingly low strikeout total of 34.

The Cardinals, though leaps and bounds better than they had been in years— if ever—still had trouble drawing fans to Robison Field. On June 1, the federal government started enforcing an additional ten percent war tax on each ticket sold, and with a wartime thriftiness, St. Louis residents avoided spending too much on diversions like baseball. By the end of the season, less than 1,000 fans attended each game. Rickey took the opportunity to build a young fan base by establishing the Knothole Gang, which gave free passes to poor youngsters from around the city. In addition, though Huggins and company were securely in third place for most of the season, they never presented a serious challenge to John McGraw's New York Giants and finished fifteen games behind. Anyone who came to Robison Field that season came to investigate young Hornsby. For that reason and because visiting teams received a healthy share of gate receipts, Rickey was able to use his savvy thriftiness to turn a losing season into a modestly profitable one for the team's shareholders.

Since the spring, when owners had instituted the military drills as part of training camp, the first World War had threatened to derail the 1917 season. Aside from the tempered enthusiasm of paying observers, though, there had been little tangible effect on the games themselves. The American commitment to the war would reach its peak the next year, however, and as able-bodied men and citizens of an exceptionally patriotic era, scores of major league players were enlisting. Those who chose not to enlist off the bat were subject to the draft. With quality players shipping out to war every day, baseball's owners agreed to reduce the roster requirement to twenty-one men and to cut their spring training schedules in half.

Hornsby appeared before his draft board in Fort Worth to receive his eligibility classification in January 1918. In late May, Hornsby's brother William had been shot and killed in a barroom fight and a few weeks later his mother had fallen ill with an unknown but chronic sickness. He pleaded with the board that as the only unmarried male in his family, his income provided the sole support for his mother and sister. He received a Class 3 deferment, which meant he could continue to play baseball indefinitely.

Using his importance to his family and to the Cardinals as leverage, Hornsby armed himself for one of the inevitable contract squabbles that he and Rickey were making a winter routine. Rickey had proposed that Hornsby repeat his salary from the season before, but Hornsby was aware of the profits he had earned his team and his enviable status as a draft-exempt ballplayer. He also really *was* the sole support of his mother and sister, and he had asked Sarah Martin, the young Denison woman he had courted since before Connery bought him for the big leagues, to marry him. He requested $7,000. Rickey knew his young star was valuable but stayed firmly within his budget for what would surely be a fiscally hopeless season. Hornsby finally agreed to the contract he'd sought a year before: $4,000 per season for two years.

Throughout Hornsby's short experience with the Cardinals, there had been very little continuity in his team's roster. Young players were bought and sold to minor league teams frequently, Roy Corhan had come and gone, and veterans who cost too much or played too poorly were released. The war promised to decimate the team's lineup. The upcoming season was to be the first time in his National League career, however, that Rogers would play for a manager other than Miller Huggins.

The abrupt righting of the St. Louis ship in 1917 had brought national attention to Huggins as a manager who could handle young players. Colonel James Ruppert, owner of the New York Yankees, liked the diminutive Huggins' wise and fiery style. The colonel had his friend Taylor Spink of the *Sporting News* offer Huggins a large contract to take control of the Yankees. Rickey, who had mended his feud with Huggins by refusing to interfere with the manager's command of the clubhouse, pleaded with the popular Huggins on his players' behalf, but could not match the money offered. Huggins left for New York.[17]

Hornsby never took a liking to the man Rickey hired to replace Huggins. Jack Hendricks was a 43-year-old graduate of Northwestern University who, like

Rickey, had played sparingly in his two major league seasons more than a decade before. He had caught Rickey's eye as a successful minor league manager and was the first choice to succeed Huggins. Hendricks first met Hornsby when, just after he was hired, Hendricks went to Fort Worth as Rickey's proxy to discuss the shortstop's contract. Hornsby shunned him, saying he would talk only to Rickey, and a cold animosity between the two set in permanently. Three reasons contributed to Hornsby's distaste for his new manager: Rogers was now a big star, naturally ornery with a growing ego; he was a high school dropout who distrusted higher education his entire life; and he had come to love Huggins, who had a law degree from the University of Cincinnati but, unlike Rickey and Hendricks, had played professional baseball for a long time and managed with a player's mentality.

The 1918 season was hard on Hendricks, hard on Hornsby, and hard on the Cardinals. Player after player was called to active duty in Europe, Hornsby played the worst season of his major league career, and the team demonstrated their hardship by sinking back to last place. Hornsby suffered injuries to his groin, his shoulder, and his thumb. He sat out games and when he did play, he either failed to hit or complained of his teammates' failures. Hendricks began to say publicly that he thought Hornsby wasn't giving his all to the team. The manager complained to Rickey. He even fined his star fifty dollars for getting tagged out at home plate standing up instead of sliding. Hornsby's indignant response, though he paid the fine, was "I'm too good a ballplayer to be sliding for a tailend team," a comment which did little to smooth his relationship with fellow players who thought him arrogant.[18] Hendricks, either cowed by Hornsby's intemperance or by Rickey's demand for a peaceful locker room, decided to return the money.

The Cardinals were 24–37 at the end of June when the United States government declared that baseball should proceed as normally as possible, but should end the season early, on Labor Day. News also came from the draft board that Hornsby's status had been changed. He was reclassified as eligible for service, which meant that like scores of other players, he either had to take up a war-essential occupation or enter the military. He agreed to take work in the shipyards of Wilmington, Delaware as soon as the season ended. Hornsby played out the schedule with St. Louis and finished with the best stats on the team by a fair margin. His .281 average, though higher than any of his teammates', was considerably lower than he was accustomed to hitting. It also gave his critics on the team ammunition for their claims that he was as responsible as anyone for their 51–78 record (thirty-three games behind the pennant-winning Cubs).

While Rickey oversaw the hasty resolution of the end-of-season business, the Harlan Shipyards in Delaware awaited Hornsby's services. The team president, one of the few individuals active in the club's daily business who still considered Hornsby a friend by the end of the 1918 season, wished the young star luck and set about preparing himself to go to war. The 37-year-old Rickey, well-educated, successful, comfortable in his family life, and beginning to gain some of his midlife heft, felt compelled by patriotic feeling and personal philosophy to join the military effort in Europe. The U.S. Army commissioned him as a major and put him in charge of a unit devoted to gas warfare.

Rickey, serving in the unit alongside Captains Ty Cobb and Christy Mathewson and Lieutenant George Sisler, arrived in France in late September and set to work instructing enlisted men about defense against mustard gas attacks. Meanwhile, Rogers Hornsby was honeymooning in Philadelphia before going to work as a plate-setter in the shipyards and as the best player on Harlan's baseball team. When he learned that he was not going to have to serve in the war, Hornsby had arranged with his fiancée Sarah to meet in Philadelphia. She met him there on September 22, and they married in a civil ceremony the next day. After a few days he had to report to Wilmington to begin his wartime job; he earned $400 per month, and very little was actually asked of him other than that he win ballgames in the shipyard league.

He and his new bride did not have to stay in Delaware long, though, as the Great War ended sooner than most expected and "war-essential" jobs were no longer required. Armistice in Europe was declared on November 11, 1918. Mr. and Mrs. Hornsby returned to Fort Worth within the month, where they rented a house near his mother's. Hornsby went to work as an automobile salesman and recuperated from what had become a long season of baseball.

Back quickly from his command in France, Branch Rickey settled himself at his home in Lucasville, Ohio to recuperate from the war and to prepare the Cardinals for what was expected to be an important year for the major leagues. For that reason, the months leading up to the 1919 season began what became an almost annual offseason debate: how much money was Rogers Hornsby worth to a baseball team?

NOTES

1. Earl Obenshain, editor of the *Sporting News* at the time, quoted in the *St. Louis Post-Dispatch*, April 1916.
2. Clipping, May 1917. Rogers Hornsby Collection, National Baseball Library, Cooperstown, NY.
3. Clipping, *St. Louis Post-Dispatch*, July 1916. Rogers Hornsby Collection, National Baseball Library, Cooperstown, NY.

4. Hornsby, *My Kind of Baseball*, 37.

5. Rogers Hornsby and Bill Surface, *My War with Baseball* (New York: Coward-McCann, 1962), 38.

6. The St. Louis Stars, the city's Negro League entry, also played competitive and entertaining baseball for many years. However, the city's white residents—and its major newspapers—barely acknowledged the team's existence.

7. The Terriers, managed by Fielder Jones and led offensively by 22-year-old St. Louis native Jack Tobin, finished 87–67 in 1915, one half game behind Federal League champion Chicago.

8. Murray Polner, *Branch Rickey: A Biography* (New York: Atheneum, 1982), 72.

9. Peter Golenbock, *The Spirit of St. Louis: A History of the St. Louis Cardinals and Browns* (New York: Spike, 2000), 69–70.

10. Undated clipping, *Sporting News* [1916?]. Rogers Hornsby Collection, The Sporting News Archives, St. Louis.

11. "Robins Have Sport With Feeble Cards," *New York Times*, September 23, 1916, 8.

12. "Best Youngster in National," *Sporting News*, July 13, 1916.

13. Ibid.

14. Clipping, *St. Louis Post-Dispatch*, July 1916. Rogers Hornsby Collection, National Baseball Library, Cooperstown, NY.

15. Alexander, *Rogers Hornsby*, 32–33.

16. Polner, *Branch Rickey: A Biography*, 74.

17. Well-founded rumors circulated that American League president Ban Johnson pressured Ruppert to hire Huggins away from the Cardinals as revenge on Rickey for switching leagues in St. Louis the year before.

18. *Sporting News*, September 5, 1918, 6.

MONEY

At the beginning of the first season after World War I, any team in the National League would have been happy to have Rogers Hornsby in their lineup. The country was relieved that the war had ended successfully and was ready to return to their favorite diversion. No player in the league held as much promise for continued development as Hornsby, and his presence would provide a tremendous means to capitalize on the postwar influx of paying fans. Murray Polner, a biographer of Branch Rickey, explains that the period after the war was the "Golden Age of Sports": the decade to come would be an "euphoric ten years sparked by higher real income and reduced working hours. Together with the development of radio and the mushrooming of automobiles, they spelled prosperity for baseball."[1] However, in 1919, the Cardinals were still a very poor team, which forced Rickey to at least consider offers for his best player.

Charles Weeghman, the owner of the Chicago Cubs, keenly understood the difference Hornsby could make at the box office. Weeghman, the former Federal League owner who nearly lured Walter Johnson to his Chicago Whales, had signed Grover Cleveland Alexander, the great Philadelphia Phillies' pitcher, in 1918. He was attempting to draw large crowds with Alexander's first full season in Chicago. Weeghman also knew that adding his league's premier offensive star would make his team as attractive to Chicagoans as the talented White Sox, led by "Shoeless" Joe Jackson. He had been rebuffed by the Cardinals for two consecutive offseasons, but he reminded Branch Rickey that he was still offering $75,000 in cash for Hornsby. Again in 1919, Rickey declined Weeghman's proposal.

Rogers Hornsby, in a redesigned Cardinals uniform, 1922. *National Baseball Hall of Fame Library, Cooperstown, N.Y.*

John McGraw had managed the New York Giants for nearly two decades, and in that time he had won six pennants and one world championship, establishing himself alongside Connie Mack as one of the great team leaders in the game. He had also achieved a reputation as an almost impeccable evaluator of baseball talent. By selecting men for the Giants that would play hard, would limit their mistakes, and wouldn't balk at his blunt and sometimes scathing criticisms, he built competitive teams year after year. His substantial overtures toward obtaining Hornsby most piqued Rickey's interest. However, it also confirmed his belief that the Cardinals must retain their star, for if McGraw wanted Hornsby so badly, the player was definitely worth keeping.

Beginning in 1919, McGraw and new Giants majority owner Charles Stoneham regularly approached Rickey with generous offers for Hornsby—offers that would have eased St. Louis's financial hardships considerably. Rickey resisted. He knew that an infusion of cash would help give him the necessary funds to sign quality veteran players that the Cardinals needed to make an immediate improvement. He also believed, however, that with a star like Hornsby as a cornerstone, he might assemble a team of young players that would grow into a winner. His plans to establish a "farm system" of minor league teams that the Cardinals would stock with developing youths they had under contract and his aggressive—and inexpensive—attempts to find major league talent through open tryouts were strategies that other major league teams had yet to consider. Born of financial necessity, Rickey's innovations would eventually make St. Louis a perennial contender for the pennant and one of the most efficient organizations in baseball.

The team president's prescriptions for the immediate future were somewhat less successful. Dissension in the locker room had compounded the Cardinals woes in 1918; unhappy and unskilled players made the outlook for their on-field performance in 1919 just as bleak. Hendricks and many of Hornsby's teammates felt that Rickey and the Cardinals organization coddled their star. In turn, Hornsby increased his public criticisms of Hendricks. He said that if Hendricks was to be the Cardinals manager for a second season, he would rather that Rickey traded him to another team. When a reporter suggested the possibility of Rickey taking over as field manager in Hendricks's place, Hornsby enthusiastically replied that he would "be out there giving the best that's in me."[2]

The Cardinals board of directors, likely influenced by Hornsby's statements but more so by Hendricks's stewardship of a last place effort, decided to release the manager from his contract late in January 1919. Rickey was installed as his replacement as predicted, a move that saved the team the need to pay a manager's salary. The transition furthered the perception among the team that management was too quick to appease Hornsby. The 23-year-old star was the team's statistical leader and fan favorite, but as a teammate he would be neither a leader nor a favorite that season.

Rickey was also growing impatient with Hornsby's status. He liked the young man and admired his skills, but he wearied of the routine contract discussion and felt strong pressure from the stockholders to keep Hornsby happy. He even complained to reporters that the very generous and very public offers that Weeghman and McGraw were making had inflated Hornsby's sense of his value, making it impossible to negotiate a sensible contract. The flaunting of their teams' wealth and interest in Hornsby, Rickey would repeat several times, "wrought damage" to the Cardinals and "made the player dissatisfied" with his current situation.[3] Hornsby was no doubt valuable; he did not, however, warrant the $10,000 salary he desired. There would be no raise at all for Hornsby this off-season, for his performance and behavior the previous year gave him little other than newspaper reports of the Cubs and Giants offers to negotiate with.

Because of the team's financial hardships, Rickey decided not to take his players south for spring training. They trained instead at Washington University in St. Louis. This was a disappointment to Rickey, who believed warm weather was conducive to conditioning and morale, and to Hornsby, who loved returning to the field for the first time each year in his beloved Texas.

Hornsby and Rickey actually made a harmonious on-field pair that season. Though Hornsby had played all but three games in the previous two seasons at shortstop, he did not flinch when Rickey decided that John "Doc" Lavan, a veteran from the American League, would play the position in 1919 and that Hornsby would move to third. He also refused to complain as Rickey moved him around the field and the line-up as the manager sought to take advantage of pitching matchups and opponents' weaknesses. A few years before, Hornsby had earned respect by his willingness to play any position. As an established star in 1919, he practically did just that: he played seventy-two games at third base that season, in addition to thirty-seven at shortstop, twenty-five at second base, and five at first base. The rotation actually improved his fielding, as he made only 34 errors and developed confidence at each position, particularly second base. Rickey took note.

Even the strongest of Hendricks' supporters were curious to play for the inventive Rickey, willingly adopting his unusual defensive schemes and line-up changes. Results were not as positive. The team opened the season in Cincinnati and Chicago, losing their first five and ten of their first twelve games. Rickey tinkered with his players' positioning, his pitching rotation, and his batting order, but aside from an impressive 16–5 stretch in early June, the 1919 Cardinals were a complete disappointment. The finished 54–83 and escaped last place only because the Phillies were even more inept.

Rogers Hornsby had returned to form offensively, however, which was a relief to Rickey and other Hornsby supporters, and he had hustled with his former vigor, satisfying teammates whom he'd alienated the season before. Those teammates failed to capitalize on the opportunities his bat created; his .318 average, 68 runs, and 68 RBIs led the team by a wide margin. Rickey the team president knew that the only way for Rickey the field manager to succeed was to shore up the roster surrounding his only consistent hitter. For the Cardinals and the whole of major league baseball, the 1919–1920 offseason would be among the busiest and most meaningful in history.

The World Series between the Chicago White Sox and the Cincinnati Reds was generating massive attention across the country, particularly for two teams from the western reaches of the major leagues. Fervor for the first post-war Series was so great that league presidents Ban Johnson and John Heydler agreed to extend the contest to a best-of-nine format. Interest was also at an all-time high in the gambling community; the attention there was curiously centered on the Reds. The betting against Chicago—a 3–1 favorite—was actually so heavy that on the day before the Series opened, bookmakers felt compelled to adjust their lines, as Cincinnati abruptly became the 8–5 favorite. Rumors of a fix swirled when New York gambler Arthur Rothstein place a huge sum on the Reds, but once the games were underway, the talk quieted and an exciting series ensued.[4]

Led by Edd Roush, who had edged out Hornsby for the league batting title, Cincinnati jumped out to a 4–1 series advantage. The whispers circulated again, and when Chicago owner Charley Comiskey approached Heydler and Johnson with suspicions, Johnson publicly scoffed at the idea of a fix. Even though seven White Sox were in fact being paid to sabotage their team's chances, Chicago won two games in a row, including a masterful pitching performance in game seven by ace Ed Cicotte, who had committed to the fix. Game eight, however, was set for the Reds; one gambler was quoted saying "It's going to be the biggest first inning you ever saw."[5] Sox pitcher Lefty Williams complied, surrendering four runs in the first inning of a 10–5 Reds win.

Before Cincinnati won the championship Rogers and Sarah Hornsby were already back in Fort Worth, which they still considered their permanent home, to help care for his mother, who was again ill. Though in future years he would make a point to attend as many World Series games as he could, he followed the 1919 contest and rumors only through newspaper reports. He took little notice of the controversy and made few comments other than expressing a slight doubt that Joe Jackson and his teammates would agree to willingly give up baseball's ultimate prize.

The news that Rogers surely found more interesting than rumors of cheating came just after the new year began. Ty Cobb was undoubtedly still the biggest star in baseball, but in 1919 another American League star emerged who would eventually surpass Cobb and every other player in fame and accomplishment. In the first season in which he played more than 100 games, George Herman "Babe" Ruth of the Boston Red Sox had hit an astounding 29 home runs, the major league record by a wide margin and nearly three times that of any other player. In contrast Hornsby, considered a powerful hitter in his own right, hit 8 home runs that season. Ruth began his career as a fearsome pitcher, but the bat of the 26-year-old southpaw made it a necessity that he play every day. One season as a full-time left fielder made him a hitter feared more than Sisler, Hornsby, and even Cobb. The desire of Miller Huggins and Colonel Ruppert of the Yankees for a hard-hitting outfielder soon made "baseball's greatest attraction" its most expensive player as well.[6]

Ruppert and Red Sox owner Harry Frazee, looking to finance pet projects outside of baseball but also insisting that Boston "could no longer put up with [Ruth's] eccentricities,"[7] agreed that the Yankees would pay $125,000 for the Babe, who had a two year contract worth $10,000 per season. The Yankees doubled his salary. The fee paid for Ruth and his new contract were the two largest of their kind in baseball's history, and arguably the greatest bargain in the history of professional sports.

The huge money directed toward Ruth gave Hornsby ammunition as he once again negotiated a new contract with St. Louis. He had never had a season like Ruth's, but consistently he had been far ahead of his league offensively; plus, while the American League had Ruth, Cobb, Jackson, Sisler, Tris Speaker, and Eddie Collins, Rogers Hornsby was easily the senior circuit's most recognizable name. The 1917 retirement of Honus Wagner had cast Hornsby as one of the lone offensive attractions of the National League, with players like Roush, Heinie Groh, and Ross Youngs as his peers. The Ruth extravaganza convinced Hornsby that not only the Cardinals but the whole league relied on his fame. He wanted a superstar's salary. He wouldn't get one in 1920.

He would earn more money than he ever had before, however. Though there were rumors that he had received a three-year contract worth $25,000, he signed a contract late in January that paid only $5,000 for the season, a raise of 25 percent rather than 100 percent. The magical figure of $10,000 had not even been considered by the Cardinals organization, but Hornsby felt he had made headway with the club. He managed to spin the news of his contract in his own favor, insisting that he wanted to be paid what he was worth but also was just anxious to play baseball. The "biggest salary" of his career would definitely coincide with "my biggest year to date."[8] For his part, Rickey's perception of the trade offers' effect on Hornsby's ego changed: commending Hornsby's willingness to consider the team's financial situation, he said, "All this talk about offers ranging upward to in the neighborhood of $100,000 have reached his ears, but he has no inflated idea as to his value."[9]

Branch Rickey had a new ally in his efforts to keep the franchise financially conservative. Sam Breadon, a St. Louis millionaire who held about fifty shares (less than two percent) in the team, had taken over as team president when he loaned the board of directors $18,000 in January 1920. The sudden transition, which necessitated the demotion of Rickey to vice president, at first hurt the manager-president's pride and he considered resigning. When the board decided that Breadon would receive 72 percent ownership in the team as repayment for the loan and that a majority of the remainder would transfer to Rickey, he was placated. The two men would never become close friends, but their working relationship would successfully survive a few fluctuations to last for many years.

Like Phil Ball with the Browns, Breadon was unimpressed by Rickey's religious constitution and erudite character but came to trust his baseball genius almost completely. In turn, Rickey admired the business acumen of the self-made man but considered his short temper unbecoming and personal habits less than scrupulous. Breadon was a grade school dropout from New York City who had moved west in 1900 and become wealthy as an automobile dealer, eventually the largest distributor of Fords in Missouri. He had amassed his fortune by selling his product to a large number of customers and spending little himself, a philosophy he tried to apply to the Cardinals.

Rickey agreed with the concept, though on occasion he had to pry money from Breadon's tight fist in order to improve his roster. Because they had won their battle with Hornsby, Breadon did relent enough to allow Rickey to buy the contract of minor league pitcher Jesse Haines, a twenty-game winner at Kansas City, and to trade a number of players for veteran first baseman Jack Fournier, whom Rickey hoped would provide the necessary offensive support for Hornsby.

The business decision Breadon faced was whether Hornsby would yield more income for the organization at the ticket office or on the trading block. Lingering debt in the organization and the huge sums Frazee had elicited from Ruppert made the latter seem like the wiser option. Breadon was brazen, but would not go over Rickey's head, who still favored keeping his young friend.

Beginning in December of 1919 before his annual vacation in Cuba, John McGraw had resumed his aggressive pursuit of the Cardinals third baseman. The Giants had lost a number of position players through retirements, injuries, and trades and were left with the promising second baseman Frankie Frisch as their only reliable infielder. McGraw felt he needed Hornsby more than ever.

Before he left for Havana, McGraw telegrammed St. Louis with an offer of four players and $70,000. Rickey declined and made no counteroffer. By February, after the Ruth sale, Rickey and Breadon had rejected an increased offer and again reiterated, this time to the press, that Hornsby was not available. New York sportswriters began to speculate on alternative solutions McGraw might create. Boston shortstop Rabbit Maranville became the center of the new rumors in the Manhattan papers while the *St. Louis Post-Dispatch* and Cardinals fans, who had gone so far as to petition Breadon and Rickey against a Hornsby trade, declared victory.

The team reported to Brownsville, Texas for spring training, and the manager announced that, given Hornsby's demonstrated flexibility and Milt Stock's experience as a third baseman, Hornsby would play this season at second base. While many of the Cardinals crossed the border to sample the nightlife of Matamoras, Mexico to Rickey's great dismay, he and Hornsby, both married men and non-drinkers, sat in the restaurant and lobby of their hotel and discussed the nuances of playing second night after night. Rickey's instruction was the foundation for Hornsby's consistent performance, highlighted by a lightning quick turn of the double play, at the position he would play almost every game for the remainder of his career. It can be said that, for the most part, the 1920 spring training was the last time the brash but ardent student of baseball felt he had something important to learn from a manager.

As the season opened Hornsby seemed prepared to keep his promise to have his biggest year yet. The team made a decent start, with pitcher Bill Doak in top form and the revamped lineup led by Fournier hitting much more frequently than their predecessors. However, Hornsby still earned the most attention. The new second baseman appeared comfortable in the field; at the plate, he made opposing pitchers extremely uncomfortable. At the end of May, with the Cardinals 17–22, Hornsby's batting average was .406, twenty points higher than Groh and more than thirty higher than American League leader Doc Johnston of Cleveland.

St. Louis play improved in June and they rose in the standings to second place. Meanwhile, the Giants had failed to acquire Maranville from Boston and were still weak on the left side of their infield. As McGraw watched the Cardinals pass his Giants, he thought he saw a new opportunity to wheedle Rickey. At the start of a series between the two teams, McGraw handed Rickey a lineup card that showed how Rickey's team might look if he accepted the Giants latest offer of five players and a larger sum of cash for Hornsby. Rickey was tempted by McGraw's ploy, but declined with a smile.

The owners were brought into the negotiation. Charles Stoneham offered the five Giants and $150,000, 20 percent more than Ruth's price without even considering the players. Breadon and Rickey refused. Stoneham then looked Rickey squarely in the eye and offered what St. Louis needed most: straight cash. The outrageous offer of $300,000 was larger than the total of the Cardinals considerable debt, but Rickey again declined and made a bizarre counter. He would buy the young Frankie Frisch from Stoneham and McGraw for $100,000. The Giants manager laughed and Stoneham declared that Rickey didn't even have the money to make the offer legitimate. Rickey was still shaking from the courage required to turn down such a lucrative offer, but his point was clear. The Cardinals intended to win—with Rogers Hornsby.

Rickey issued a statement from New York. "Papers have been printing daily stories about the sale of Rogers Hornsby," he said. "This is not new or unexpected, as Hornsby has been sold on several previous occasions. However, rumors are so persistent that even one club President is quoted as having become quite exercised about the sale. . . . I will say once more that Hornsby is not for sale." His message was bold for a team at their highest point in the standings in several seasons: "The Cardinals are out to win here and now. In any event, the sportsmanship of our people is not for sale."[10] Rickey surely must have felt a moment's pause, though, when Hornsby lay motionless on the ground the next day, temporarily knocked unconscious by teammate Doc Lavan's throw from shortstop.

Breadon and Rickey had made a remarkable windfall through another variety of baseball transaction and secured the financial solvency of the team in the process. Rickey convinced his former boss Phil Ball to allow the Cardinals to share Sportsman's Park, the home of the Browns, at a lease of $20,000 per year. The move allowed Breadon to dismantle Robison Field—the last fully wooden stadium structure in the major leagues—and sell a parcel of the land to the St. Louis Board of Education for $200,000 and another at $75,000 to the city's public services as a location for a streetcar station. In addition, Sportsman's Park was a better facility that could accommodate larger crowds and thus produce more ticket revenue. The money resolved all of the team's debt to Mrs. Britton and funded Rickey's pet project, the farm system experiment. Thus, one real estate transaction essentially sealed the future success and prosperity of the entire franchise.

The Cardinals began play at Sportsman's Park in July, and though their winning percentage and their place in the standings began to slip, fans bought more tickets in the latter half of 1920 than in entire seasons at Robison Field a few years before. St. Louisans were treated to a dual display of hitting prowess that year. Hornsby, slightly off from his torrid start but still rapping hits consistently to all fields, ran away with the National League batting title, while the Browns Sisler finished his season as dazzlingly as Hornsby started. Sisler won the American League title with an average better than those of Ruth, Cobb, and Speaker—and better than .400.

Cardinals fans also witnessed a remarkable pitching display at the end of the year. Cardinals rookie Jesse Haines, who appeared in a league-best forty-seven games that season, and Cubs star Grover Alexander each pitched the full 17 innings of a game on October 1. The Cubs 3–2 victory was Alexander's twenty-seventh and Haines' record, which did not indicate the quality of his major league debut, fell to 13–20.

Hornsby watched his teammates from the Cardinals bench that day, where he rested the ankle he sprained September 9 in Brooklyn, covering first on a bunt—a play the new second baseman had not quite mastered. His season ended awkwardly, but the cumulative result was remarkable. He had scored 96 times and driven in 94 runs, and besides his .370 average had also led the National League with 218 hits and 44 doubles. His team's final record of 75–79 put them in a tie for fifth place, which was not an unimpeachable success but showed that the Cardinals were learning to win under Rickey.

The organization's financial situation was secure and could possibly be considered strong. Hornsby was now not only the National League's most recognizable and promising star, but its best player. He hoped that his deference before the season would be remembered when the time came to negotiate a contract for the upcoming years. He decided that it was fair that his salary fall somewhere between that of the aging Cobb and the powerful Ruth. Three years at $18,000 per season seemed right.

He also had a new reason to seek a higher salary: he was a father. Rogers Hornsby Jr. was born in November 1920. His parents had opted not to make the return trip to Texas, but instead were looking to buy a home in or around St. Louis. Sarah Hornsby, proud of her husband's success and excited about motherhood, and Rogers agreed that it would be best to live in one place with the boy year-round. Hornsby went to work using his famous name to sell insurance in the city, but a higher baseball salary would allow his family the comforts he never had growing up near the stockyards in Fort Worth.

He negotiated directly with Breadon after his son's birth. The president would not even consider Hornsby's $54,000 demand and the pair bickered politely for two months. When Breadon fell ill in January 1921, Hornsby went to his bedside at St. John's Hospital and accepted another one-year contract. He would make $11,000 for his services in 1921, an abrupt raise of more than double his previous salary. Hornsby biographer Charles Alexander notes, however, that "each man came away feeling that the other was unappreciative of his particular circumstances."[11] Hornsby was potentially worth more than a quarter million dollars to the franchise at any one moment, but would be paid just a fraction of that for his efforts. He knew, however, that there was nothing to be done but to continue to play each year proving he was worth much more than he earned.

Tris Speaker's Cleveland Indians won the 1920 World Series over the Brooklyn Dodgers, but most of the attention in the last months of the year was focused on the losers of the preceding championship. The White Sox had finished only two games behind Cleveland in the American League (and one game ahead of the Yankees and Ruth's otherworldly total of 54 home runs). When the pennant race heated up, so had rumors that the White Sox were cheaters of the worst kind. Charley Comiskey hired private detectives to investigate the claims.

Almost immediately after the season was over, the American League filed charges of conspiring to profit from fixing the 1919 World Series against eight Chicago players, including Jackson, Williams, and Cicotte, and five gamblers in federal court. The country was shocked by the seriousness of the formal allegations. The major league owners sought to repair baseball's suddenly tarnished image and prevent similar circumstances in the future. They decided to reorganize Organized Baseball.

The position of Commissioner of Baseball replaced the previously ineffective and practically unknown three-member commission that had loosely governed professional baseball before. The Commissioner would assume ultimate decision-making authority over the major and minor leagues, with the American League and National League presidents his immediate subordinates. The owners of the major league teams voted unanimously to appoint Judge Kenesaw Mountain Landis to the post, with a salary of $50,000 per year for seven years and headquarters at an office building in Chicago.

After the minor league representatives approved the massive "constitution" of Organized Baseball, Landis formally took his post in late January 1921. The veteran judge who had ruled against the Federal League a few years before immediately went to work addressing the issues of cheating and bribery in the sport he loved. His first statement to the press as commissioner sent a firm message to the men he was selected to control. "If I catch any crook in baseball, the rest of his life is going to be a pretty hot one," he said. "I'll go to any means and do anything possible to see that he gets a real penalty for his offense."[12]

A stronger message came with his treatment of the accused White Sox. With their trial delayed to the fall and firm evidence against the players either lost or proving difficult to authenticate, Landis announced that the eight players were banned from the game, putting them on the permanently ineligible list until they could show "clear evidence" that they were not involved. He dramatically declared, "Baseball is not powerless to protect itself."[13] None of players ever achieved reinstatement, though all involved were acquitted of criminal charges in August 1921.

Landis believed gambling to be the primary enemy of fair play in baseball, and set out to eradicate even the slightest hint of it from the game. He had the rules against betting on baseball posted in every locker room and dissuaded players against entering into even the smallest stakes in cards, at the track, or on other sports. Over the coming years Hornsby, just learning the fun and money to be had picking the winners of dog and horse races, would hear the commissioner's message personally.

NOTES

1. Polner, *Branch Rickey: A Biography*, 78.

2. *Sporting News*, December 17, 1918, 24.

3. "Weeghman Verbally Pounded by Rickey for Offers to Hornsby," *New York Times*, February 14, 1918, 13.

4. Richard M. Cohen and David S. Neft, *The World Series: Complete Play-by-Play of Every Game, 1903–1985* (New York: Macmillan, 1986), 76.

5. Ibid.

6. "Ruth Bought by New York Americans for $125,000," *New York Times*, January 6, 1920, 16.

7. "Babe Ruth Accepts Terms of Yankees," *New York Times*, January 7, 1920, 22.

8. Hornsby and Surface, *My War with Baseball*, 40.

9. Alexander, *Rogers Hornsby*, 55.

10. "Hornsby Not on Market," *New York Times*, June 13, 1920, 24.

11. Alexander, *Rogers Hornsby*, 64.

12. "Judge Landis Promises Hot Time for Crooks in Baseball," *New York Times*, January 31, 1921, 16.

13. "White Sox Players Banned by Landis," *New York Times*, March 13, 1921, 16.

THE RAJAH

In 1921, Paramount Pictures released one of the most popular films of the silent-movie era, *The Sheik*. Hornsby avoided the flickering lights of movie projectors to protect his batting eyes, so it is unlikely he saw or possibly even knew of the movie, but much of the country certainly did. Starring the dashing and decidedly Italian Rudolph Valentino as a Saudi prince, the picture almost single-handedly engendered a passion for all things "Arabian" in the United States. The popularization of Middle Eastern culture in the West even found its way to the baseball stadiums, most memorably in the nicknames bestowed on the game's finest players. At a time when editors of sports columns and newsreels demanded exceptionally colorful and varied terminology from writers, nicknames came from all corners of popular culture and changed routinely until one stuck on a player.

Babe Ruth was clearly the most impressive hitter of his era after his giant 1920 season. With the release of the Valentino film, newsmen jumped on the opportunity to apply a Middle Eastern honorific on the large personality. Ruth's prowess with the bat made him the "Sultan of Swat." Of course, the dominion of Swat was large enough for several princes, and Rogers Hornsby's feats earned him a similar title in the National League. His name and his attitude directed fans and writers to a natural fit, the "Rajah of Swat." "The ease with which his first name slides into that sonorous title" was the genesis of the nickname, but he would live up to it over the next few years as he attempted to keep pace with Ruth's skill and fame.[1]

A New York sportswriter would later assess the remarkable accomplishments

Rogers Hornsby in the stands at Sportsman's Park, while recuperating from injury in 1923. *National Baseball Hall of Fame Library, Cooperstown, N.Y.*

of Hornsby in the first half of the 1920s, describing the stature he achieved in those years in terms of his nickname. "He is a prince of the diamond," Kenneth Campbell exclaimed, "and rules the imagination of baseball fans with a brash insolence as was ever displayed by an Eastern potentate."[2] Indeed, Hornsby's blunt manner and the broad swath of his public criticisms became the personality traits he was known for; fame, however, he earned with his bat.

If Hornsby was considered the National League's best player after winning his first batting title in 1920, the seasons of 1921 through 1925 certified his place among the greatest ballplayers in history. The marks he set in each particular campaign are remarkable in themselves, but the cumulative effort ranks as one of the finest five-year stretches possible. In fact, his batting average in those seasons combined was .401; no other player ever achieved a similar figure over five years, not even Ty Cobb. His individual accomplishments during this run included three season averages over .400—including the highest single-season batting average of the twentieth century—and six consecutive batting titles (including 1920). He twice won the Triple Crown of highest average, most home runs, and most RBIs for one season, led his league in RBIs three times, and twice hit more home runs than even the mighty Ruth. He won a Most Valuable Player award and narrowly missed another.

Although the New York Giants won four straight pennants and two World Series without him, McGraw lusted after Hornsby year after year. Meanwhile, Rickey and Breadon watched his remarkable feats, satisfied that even the largest trade offers did not represent their star's true value. The Cardinals, bolstered by their nearly superhuman second baseman and the fruits of Rickey's player development system, were a winning franchise.

The hope for consistent success began as early as spring training in 1921, evidenced by the overcrowded stands at all the Cardinals exhibition games. Training in Orange, Texas—500 miles removed from the temptations of Matamoras—Rickey's team looked much the same as it had the season before, but with the line-up and pitching rotation building on a year's experience together, they felt confident they would improve. As a team, the Cardinals were much better, and as an organization, they were poised for profit and success. The exhibition season, including a greatly anticipated meeting between Hornsby and Ruth in Shreveport, Louisiana, and the largest crowd ever for the St. Louis City Series at Sportsman's Park, indicated that ticket buyers were ready to support the franchise.

Dramatically increased offensive production across the major leagues produced a proportionate rise in attendance at all stadiums in the early 1920s. The era of the "dead ball" was officially over, it seemed, as run production had increased by nearly a third since 1916 and home runs increased 200 percent.

Hornsby surprised himself by hitting 21 home runs in 1921 and Ruth was hitting them in scores, but even the less powerful batsmen were putting the ball out of the part consistently, as dozens of players had double-digit home run totals, unthinkable only a few years before. A new baseball had quietly been introduced by Spalding in 1920, wound more tightly with an allegedly more elastic Australian yarn. The balls were also consistently whiter and less damaged, for umpires were replacing badly scuffed balls and new stadium rules instructed that fans could keep foul balls hit into the stands, a very popular change in custom.

Sportsman's Park was home to two of the greatest beneficiaries of the lively ball in Sisler and Hornsby. That they consistently outstripped their contemporaries who enjoyed the same advantages did not go unappreciated by the St. Louis fans, however, who proudly claimed two of the major leagues' leading hitters. Both men hit near .400 all season long, Hornsby as high as .426 in June. Sisler finished the year with a .371 average, while his Cardinals counterpart fell just below the magical mark and ended at .397, the modern record for the National League. Elsewhere in town, the city's African American baseball fans were administering the nickname "Cool Papa" to 19-year-old James Bell, a speedy rookie on the St. Louis Stars who, in addition to being a steady-handed pitcher, would lead the Negro Leagues in hitting several times. At one time, the Midwestern city was home to three of the most consistent batters any of their leagues had ever seen.

Such mighty individual performers raised fans' expectations for the major league teams as well. The Browns—who had actually finished the 1910s with the worst cumulative record in the majors and were a game better than the Cardinals in 1920—bumped their record over .500. Rickey's team significantly improved their record for the second straight year. Jack Fournier provided solid support while Rickey recruit Austin McHenry had the best year of his young career with a .350 average and more than 100 RBIs. While fans set a St. Louis attendance record, the Cardinals stayed in the pennant race until September and then played a key role in eliminating the Pittsburgh Pirates from the race, thus delivering the title to McGraw and the Giants. Hornsby and company finished in third place; their 87–66 record was twelve wins better than the year before.

The result of the Cardinals fine season and their star's record-setting one was, predictably, another contract dispute. Tired of their routine one-year compromises, Hornsby, Breadon, and Rickey set out to agree to a longer term for the contract. Three years seemed agreeable to the men, but the rate of pay was naturally up for debate. Hornsby fairly thought that Ruth's contract, which paid $52,000 for 1921, warranted him a large increase over his own $11,000. He asked for $25,000, not even half of Ruth's take, but Breadon explained that St. Louis was not New York and that, for all Hornsby's fame, the Rajah of Swat did not draw the crowds and peripheral income that the Sultan did. They again compromised, signing the three-year contract at Hornsby's previous request of $18,000 annually. As usual, the Cardinals star failed to get what he thought he deserved, though like his batting average, his new salary was the highest in the National League's history. Thirty years later, Hornsby summed up his feelings on the contract negotiations, salaries of other players, and his desire to be a part of the game regardless of his income. "I would have played for nothing," he said, then qualified his statement. "If they're paying the other guy, naturally you want some, too."[3]

Hornsby was supplementing his income and keeping his young family housed in a beautifully furnished downtown St. Louis apartment by selling insurance in the city. It was a profitable enterprise for the ballplayer, whom city residents trusted on the basis of his mighty bat. But another means of capitalizing on his playing fame presented itself in the fall of 1921: barnstorming. The demand to see major league celebrities was large in reaches of the country where big-time baseball was accessible only through colorful newspaper accounts and the occasional newsreel before a motion picture. For the past few off-seasons, famous players had been participating in community games in exchange for a hefty share of the organizers' profits. Hornsby himself had picked up modest sums for games in Oklahoma and Texas during trips to see his mother. After the first of three New York–centered World Series between the Giants and the Yankees, the West Coast and a big paycheck called.

California, still three decades away from the major leagues' westward migration, were hungry for even a sample of the game's finest players. Investors rallied funds sufficient to lure a number of major leaguers to the four-team California State League, with four big stars to serve as player-managers: Hornsby in Los Angeles, Sisler in a town called Vernon, and Detroit's Harry Heilmann and Ty Cobb on separate teams in San Francisco. The games turned out to be very good, as Cobb and the Rajah battled for the batting title and the latter led the circuit with 13 home runs, but over a hurried sixty-one-game schedule, the West Coast crowds lost interest. The league lost money, but Hornsby and his peers certainly made some. For ten weeks of effort, Hornsby had all his expenses paid and earned $4,500—more than he had made with the Cardinals only three seasons before.[4]

Aside from the support of his wife and son, Hornsby had few interests on which to spend the large sums he was earning. He did enjoy automobiles and regularly traded up for a newer model; he also had considered buying a home, though the right one had never presented itself, and Sarah and Rogers Jr. seemed to him content in their relatively large apartment. His personal habits cost him little aside from his daily steak and pint of ice cream, for he spent no money on alcohol or tobacco. As a public figure, he dressed himself neatly but not luxuriously when he was out of uniform. The great expense of Rogers Hornsby's life was gambling. It was his "investment" and his vice; it would cause him more trouble in his career than it could have possibly earned him. "But," he'd rationalize to friends and reporters, "this was my money and I never thought it was anybody else's business what I did with it. Some guys spent it on liquor and night clubs. I didn't."[5]

The Rajah did not like to play cards and the notion of betting on baseball games sickened him, but he loved racing. From his first trip to a dog track, in New York in 1919 with teammate Jack Miller, he was entranced by the contests and pleasure he took in picking a winner. He would call horseracing the "best sport next to baseball . . . the sport of kings." From 1919 onward he bet with increasing frequency and measure. Hornsby loved the track but placed most of his wagers through bookies, preferably on horses. He never learned to properly read a racing form and his picks almost always came from tips that friends or fellow race fans shared with him, which served him well at times and on occasion cost him quite a lot. By 1922 he was gambling hundreds of dollars per month. He casually estimated that over his playing career he bet nearly half a million dollars and, according to his own generous calculations, ended up "about even, give or take a little." "If so," writer Jack Sher said of this claim, "the mighty Rajah was as accurate a judge of horseflesh as he was of horsehide."[6]

In the 1922 major league campaign, Sportsman's Park ticket buyers were treated to three magnificent individual accomplishments, though both pennant-hopeful squads would fall short of their team goals. The Browns and the Cardinals each fielded impressive teams that had some prognosticators predicting a Sportsman's Park World Series as a sequel to the Polo Grounds contests of 1921 between the Giants and Yankees. Sam Breadon was even caught up in the excitement of his promising team. Before the season began, he commissioned a new logo to complement the interlocking "StL" the team wore on their sleeves. For the annual preseason exhibitions against the Browns, the Redbirds took the field in their new uniforms, which featured the team nickname in script bookended by two cardinals perched on a bat. The logo would become one of the most recognizable in sports.

For his part, Rickey was concerned that his team was putting the prize ahead of the struggle. He complained that they trained as if complacent, that his "smug-faced" stars expected that winning would be easy, and that two seasons' progress might be undermined by "swell-headedness, unjustifiable swell-headedness."[7] Rickey's reservations may have had some grounding, but though his team would not win the pennant in 1922, they certainly did not regress. In mid-July the Cardinals led the National League and Hornsby had already surpassed his career-high in home runs while batting over .400. Even after learning their popular teammate Austin McHenry was quickly dying of a brain tumor, the team rallied a few winning streaks to stay in a four-team pennant race. They would ultimately finish fourth with one win less than their previous record, as McGraw's Giants qualified for another match with Miller Huggins' Yankees at the Polo Grounds.

The Browns had missed their chance at the World Series by only one game. They had compiled a 93-61 record behind their unassuming stars Ken Williams, who led both leagues in home runs (39) and runs batted in (155), and Sisler. The surprisingly fleet-footed first baseman had stolen a league-best 51 bases and finished his season with a .420 batting average; the 35-year-old Cobb was a distant second at .401. Babe Ruth had a relatively slow year in 1922, battling injury and a suspension, so while New York had the year's two best teams, St. Louis had its three best hitters.

"Hornsby Pretty Near the Whole Show in National" a *Sporting News* headline accurately declared after the season. As the New York teams separated themselves in their respective pennant races, Hornsby had continued the best season of his career right to its last day. He participated in every game that year and had a streak of five home runs in five days during the end of September. In the last game against the Cubs at Wrigley Field, after St. Louis sportswriter Jim Gould told him he needed 3 hits to finish the year over .400, he got them. Statistical guru Bill James has assessed Hornsby's accomplishments in 1922 as "the best season ever by a major league second baseman."[8] The .401 average made him the first National Leaguer to cross the elusive threshold in the twentieth century. His 250 hits were a league record, seven better than Willie Keeler's 30-year-old mark, and his 42 home runs were the most anyone besides Ruth had ever achieved. As the *Sporting News* article put it, he "stood so much by himself when it came to offensive work in the Heydler circuit that there is little else to the story."[9]

Meanwhile, a new character had entered the story of Hornsby's private life. At a dog track in Missouri on a midseason off-day, Cardinals catcher and fellow gambler Eddie Ainsmith introduced his friend to an attractive woman with reddish-brown hair and dark eyes wearing a modern, stylish dress. She was clearly a "flapper," a term coming into use to describe women who openly flouted the conservative social code of time. Her name was Mary Jeannette Pennington Hine, though she conveniently omitted "Hine" and all references to her husband John when she met the baseball star.[10] Hornsby, for his part, did little to disguise his attraction to Jeannette, as she was known, despite the fact that his own marriage was public knowledge and, at the time, fairly happy. A local attorney, reporting on the matter to Rickey the next season, said he believed that the woman was semiemployed by a local gambling house, pursued married men intentionally, and "is strictly a woman of the town and out for money."[11] In any event, Hornsby was hooked and the relationship that developed between Rogers and Jeannette would end both of their marriages in a short period of time.

After their initial meeting at the dog track, the pair became formally adulterous sometime in the fall of 1922. Their meetings were at first clandestine and infrequent—on one occasion they met in New York City—but they gradually grew bolder; he would visit her at the hat shop where she worked and she would meet him outside the clubhouse after games. The reticent Hornsby, who almost never corresponded with pen and paper, even began posting short notes of affection to his mistress, though he also used the opportunity to instruct her to maintain their secrecy.

By December, the affair was no secret to Sarah Hornsby, who hired detectives to follow her increasingly absent and inattentive husband. He had seemingly always been faithful to her until meeting Jeannette, but the passion between husband and wife had ended. He never discussed it, even in deposition in the legal matters his affair would give rise to, but as his fame, his wealth, and their family grew, Hornsby's love for his wife diminished. At the end of 1922, Sarah and Rogers Jr. departed for her mother's home in Los Angeles while John Hine, Jeannette's husband, simultaneously confronted his wife about his own suspicions.

The year that followed would be one of deteriorating and destroyed relationships for Rogers Hornsby. From his wife to his teammates to his manager, those who had trusted him questioned his commitments and felt challenged by his passion for gambling, a new woman, and his own vision for the way the Cardinals should play. His performance on the field never flagged, but his distractions off the field and his apparent unwillingness to get on it made 1923 one of the most difficult seasons in his career.

Despite the speedy and unchallenged divorce decree Jeannette Pennington received at the start of February and his own wife's distance, Hornsby chose to leave St. Louis for spring training in Bradenton, Florida earlier than any of his teammates. His affair still had to remain secret because he was, of course, still married and because John Hine was indicating that he had second thoughts about his divorce. Hine realized that the fame of his wife's new suitor might be financially advantageous, and he set out to have his divorce overturned and to file suit against Hornsby for destroying his marriage. Hine's actions late in the spring would publicly expose Hornsby as an adulterer, embarrassing the St. Louis celebrity and alienating some fans.

When training camp was finally underway, the Cardinals around Hornsby looked somewhat different from the team that had won more than eighty-five games two consecutive years. McHenry's brain cancer had mercifully ended his life the previous fall and Jack Fournier, the steady first baseman whose skills Hornsby most respected as a teammate, was traded to Brooklyn just before training began. In Fournier's place, Rickey had called up "Sunny" Jim Bottomley, one of the manager's finest farm system products. Bottomley would be a great player for the Cardinals, even in 1923, but in spring training that year, Hornsby felt that his team lacked its former promise.

The new line-up certainly did nothing to slow Hornsby's tremendous streak at the plate. The stress of carrying on a furtive romance and seeing his son removed from his home had caused him to lose a few pounds off the solid frame he'd maintained since his "farming out" eight years before, but his quick, level stroke was as strong as ever. As he had for more than two seasons, Hornsby played every day and, from the third spot in the line-up, hit successfully four out of every ten times at bat. But two days after his 2 home runs in a 16–4 victory over Chicago helped the team push its record over .500 for the first time that year, Hornsby sprained his knee turning one of the double plays at which he had become famously adept. He had to sit out as his team scored 80 runs in eight games. He had played almost 350 consecutive games until missing the May 9 game against Philadelphia.

He tried to return to the line-up prematurely ten days later, but after a few ineffective games, Rickey dispatched his best player back to St. Louis for medical attention. While he was in a plaster cast immobilizing his left knee, Hornsby's team lost consistently and his personal life underwent a flurry of changes. In the course of just a few weeks he would be divorced, his mistress would stay divorced, his mother would come close to death, and he would begin a long and destructive feud with his ballclub.

The day he returned to St. Louis, newspapers reported the story of his involvement with Jeannette and that he had been named in Hine's case to overturn the divorce. Confronted by reporters on May 25 as he limped off the train, he told them, "I cannot say anything, as I haven't heard anything about this matter," then cryptically indicated he might issue a statement "later."[12] Then, on June 12, Sarah Martin Hornsby's divorce petition was granted without an objection or an appearance by her former husband. At his room at the Jefferson Hotel in St. Louis, Hornsby accepted the news that his wife had been granted a $25,000 settlement and custody of their son with little emotion other than to indicate he would always provide for his son. Three days after the divorce, Hornsby's sister wired him that his mother was gravely ill. He immediately departed for Fort Worth.

In his absence, the Cardinals had started off by winning six consecutive games, but, as John McGraw correctly observed, they were "a different team when Hornsby [was] out of the game."[13] They slipped from second to sixth place while their second baseman was out of the line-up. Even when he returned to playing regularly, in late June, the team barely recovered. With his injury healed sufficiently, the Rajah had returned to his now typical level of play. He would not manage to rise back above a .400 average that season, but consistently stayed between .380 and .390 over the 107 games in which he appeared, his .384 final average good enough for his fourth straight batting title. Aside from Bottomley, who hit .371 in his first season, and Milt Stock's team-best 96 runs batted in, the Cardinals had little support for Hornsby, though. They managed to return their record to .500 and won impressively at times, but Rickey's squad was an inconsistent bunch in 1923, a trait which frustrated Hornsby—and no doubt Rickey—immensely.

The frustrations of his private life, compounded by his team's mediocrity, led Hornsby to turn on the man who had enthusiastically stewarded him through the best years of his career. Though his personnel decisions as vice president did account for it, Rickey could hardly control his players' talent from the dugout and Hornsby felt that the manager's scheming was a detriment to the team. On several occasions, the star made open and dramatic expressions of exasperation after Rickey's decisions cost the team runs; in August, Rickey could take no more. In the showers after a close loss, Hornsby complained to Ainsmith about Rickey's decision to pitch one of his young "projects" in a difficult situation. Rickey overheard the comment and, when Hornsby was leaving the locker room, reprimanded the player for his remarks. Hornsby's vulgar reply enraged the Methodist manager, and the normally peaceful Rickey swung at Hornsby. The two grappled until Rickey could be restrained.

The aftermath was as ugly as the scuffle. Rickey's pride was hurt after his loss of control, and his feelings were damaged because the young man he thought of as a friend seemed to have turned on him. Rumors immediately popped up that Hornsby was on the trading block. Even the definitive voice of Sam Breadon failed to dissuade the writers of their beliefs that either the Cubs, emboldened by the wealth of new owner William Wrigley and the resolve of president William Veeck Sr., or the Giants would have Hornsby by season's end. Meanwhile, Hornsby's friend Ainsmith, who drank as much as he gambled, was unceremoniously sold to Brooklyn after an embarrassing public display of drunkenness.

The animosity between Hornsby and the Cardinals organization was at a fever pitch. In September, Hornsby began to complain about a rash on his chest and then about aches in his knee and pulled himself from the line-up accordingly. His teammates thought he was "dogging it"; Rickey felt certain Hornsby was dodging games out of spite; Breadon was convinced that his star was intentionally undermining the team. On September 27 the owner angrily suspended Hornsby for the season's final five games and fined him $500.

When Hornsby declared the next day that he loved being in St. Louis but never wanted to play under Rickey again, he raised suspicions that he had actually been attempting to force a trade. He closed his statement to the press saying that he would "simply await developments."[14] Rickey refused to take the bait. The usually loquacious manager and vice president made a few comments on his team as a whole, about to finish over .500 but in fifth place, then addressed Hornsby's situation by concluding, "Hornsby will not be gratified by being traded."[15]

Hornsby and Rickey had been friends, though casually and oddly matched, for several years, but they had severely strained their relationship in 1923. Further, without the responsibility of a family to actively care for, Hornsby now felt he could move from St. Louis with little burden. The second baseman had made a new friend in John McGraw over the past few seasons, and it is likely that he was now hungry for the opportunity to play for the legendary manager. "Little Napoleon," as McGraw was known, shared Hornsby's blunt manner and vulgar tongue, love of baseball, and love of horseracing. In fact, the two placed bets together routinely when the Giants and Cardinals met, before venturing out for a pair of steaks after games.

Some fifty years later, a man named John Horgan recalled his days as a Giants batboy in the Polo Grounds and the special tasks McGraw had him perform. "My principle errand for McGraw was to find out who won what race. He and Rogers Hornsby had me running back and forth to the old clubhouse which was in center field. If their horses won, I would wave a white sweatshirt. If they lost, I waved a red sweatshirt which McGraw kept especially for that purpose. Both McGraw and Hornsby were crazy about the horses."[16] While some St. Louis voices called out that McGraw was tampering with their team by attempting to lure Hornsby to New York, the rumors of this game-time gambling activity were catching the attention of Commissioner Landis, who privately seethed at the legal but unseemly behavior.

Despite the firm stance they showed to the press, Rickey and Breadon did consider trading the Rajah that offseason. For the first time in the player's career, management approached other teams to test the waters on a trade. Chicago and New York were the obvious targets. Throughout the final months of 1923, Rickey met with Veeck and Cubs manager Bill Killefer several times while simultaneously carrying on discussions with Giants representatives. In both cases, however, the Cardinals manager got cold feet when negotiations reached the point where a trade was possible. He increased the amount of cash he requested from Chicago to go along with the players they offered, and the Cubs balked at the suddenly huge price tag. With New York, Rickey insisted that the deal include Frankie Frisch, whom both he and McGraw felt was a smart player with a big future, despite the fact that the Giants had stated from the start of trade talks that Frisch was one player they simply would not sacrifice.

A final temptation came at the winter owners' meetings in Chicago, when Brooklyn's Charles Ebbets approached Breadon and offered a $275,000 check in exchange for Hornsby, on the spot. Breadon, shocked, said no.[17] The Cardinals had decided not to give up the National League's best player, regardless of how large a pain his phantom ailments and egotistical disdain for authority had become in the organization. Rogers Hornsby, whose contract bound him to play for St. Louis or for no one at all, held little sway in the matter.

When it came time to play baseball again, however, Hornsby was ready to put the previous season and its troubles behind him. Perhaps a winter spent losing a huge investment in a failed Christmas tree vendor and trying to keep his infamous relationship with Jeannette Pennington out of the papers humbled him, for he reported to Breadon's offices in February ready to make amends. The star, the manager, and the owner met and reconciled—Rickey would describe it as "a settlement or whatever you call it"—all three agreeing to put the previous animosity behind them for the sake of winning.[18] Hornsby's feelings were further assuaged by restitution of the money he had been fined and had lost by not participating in a few exhibition games.

He was set to depart for spring training in Bradenton on the last day of February when he felt compelled to settle the other turbulent element of his life in 1923. His former wife and his son were far off in Los Angeles and all of John Hine's legal ministrations had finally subsided; Hornsby felt ready to marry again. He asked Jeannette to be his wife. She agreed and, with the help of his lawyer Frank Quinn, they were quickly and quietly married by a judge during the jury deliberation of a civil court trial.[19] A night at Hornsby's rooms in the Jefferson Hotel sufficed as a honeymoon, and on March 1 the ballplayer boarded a train for Florida as his wife and their lawyer set out to buy and furnish a home for the newlyweds.

St. Louis was almost solely centered on Rogers Hornsby in 1924. While the Browns and the Cardinals struggled to win and George Sisler, recovering from injuries that kept him out all the previous season, failed to register even a .300 average, Hornsby was engaged in an historic accomplishment. The batting record he set that season would turn attention from New York City's Sultan to the Rajah of St. Louis and, for at least that one season, convince the world that Hornsby was a hitter better even than his idols Cobb and Honus Wagner. His average of .424 in 1924 was higher than those three men, or Sisler, or any hitter before or after Hornsby's day would ever achieve in the modern form of baseball.

In a memoir he published a year before his death, Hornsby would assess his remarkable season with severe modesty. His entry on the year begins, "*1924—Hustled on everything I hit.*" He acknowledges that to reach the lofty figure of .424 "you have to be a little lucky," then simply notes that "the Cardinals came in sixth," finishing the entry.[20] The modesty he displayed throughout his life belied the pride Hornsby felt while bettering Napoleon Lajoie's 23-year-old modern record.[21] As crowds across the country turned out to their home parks whenever the Cardinals came to play, Hornsby graciously tipped his cap at the end of each game.

He rarely disappointed. Over sixty games in July and August, he had 106 hits in 218 at bats, an average of .486; in the entire month of August he actually hit successfully in more than half of his at-bats. He missed eleven games due to a hand injury near the beginning of the season, but through the 143 games he played, he went hitless only 24 times and never more than two games in a row.[22] Over the course of the entire historic season, Hornsby reached base more often than he failed to, finishing with an on-base percentage of .507.

Observers around the major leagues lauded Hornsby, saying that he had taken the science of hitting to a new level. Writer John Sheridan, a forty-year veteran of the *Sporting News*, decided that the Cardinals second baseman "probably is the greatest hitter of all time."[23] National League president John Heydler was more certain; in his admittedly biased opinion, his league's best player was also "the greatest batsman of all time."[24] His hitting prowess, complemented by his vocal belief that most umpires did a difficult job well, even won him praise from the men in blue. During an at-bat in Brooklyn, Hornsby had fouled off two pitches and taken two balls, when the young pitcher Jim Elliott threw a pitch he felt certain was strike three. Umpire Charles "Cy" Pfirman, who was the only man ever to throw Hornsby out of a game for arguing, called it a ball. Elliott glared at Pfirman while Hornsby tapped dirt from his cleats. On the full-count pitch, Hornsby homered to right field. As the Redbirds star circled the bases, Pfirman walked to the mound with a new baseball and a piece of advice for Elliott. "You see," the umpire told the pitcher, "Mr. Hornsby will let you know whenever your pitch is in the strike zone."[25]

A new prize was also announced. The Baseball Writers Association of America (BBWAA) had decided to award a Most Valuable Player award in the National League (the American League MVP had been so honored since 1922). Writers would vote for the award, ranking the league's best from one to ten. Hornsby seemed assured of the plaque and the accompanying 1,000 silver dollars, but when the votes were tallied, Brooklyn pitcher Dazzy Vance was named MVP. St. Louis sportswriters were furious; Cincinnati scribe Jack Ryder had left Hornsby off his ballot altogether on the grounds that the great hitter was "a most valuable player to himself, but not to his team," which had its worst season in five years.[26] Vance won the vote with seventy-four points to Hornsby's sixty-two, but none of the angry columns decrying the harm done to Hornsby noted that even if Ryder had voted Hornsby first and Vance second, Dazzy would have finished with 73 points to the Rajah's 72.

Hornsby's teammate Bill Doak corroborated Ryder's opinion. Doak went on the record saying that though Hornsby was more serious about baseball than anyone he had played with, the pitcher did not "recall that he ever showed any undue hustle and any great concern whether we won or lost. In fact, he never seemed to think of anything but his hitting."[27] Still, a litany of supporters vocally defended Hornsby as their most valued player. Rickey and McGraw both laughed off the notion that Vance was a better player than Hornsby, and writers had material for their baseball columns throughout the quiet off-season. Hornsby was diplomatic and expressed nothing but admiration for Vance, who had won twenty-eight games and was the only pitcher to strike Rajah out three times in one game. Breadon, who issued no public statement, did reward his most valuable player with a gigantic new contract. Hornsby was to earn $100,000 over the next three seasons.

With personal success, more money than he had ever imagined he would earn, and stability in his personal life, Hornsby started to think about his future. Perhaps spending his entire career in St. Louis was desirable, particularly if he might be able to continue on after his playing days as manager, something he believed "every player hopes some day" to do.[28] His former wife was set to remarry in February 1925, and his new bride was pregnant with Hornsby's second child. He and Jeannette sold the house outside of town, which made her lonely, and invested in an apartment building back in downtown St. Louis, occupying one of the flats. He was in the process of buying a farm in the Missouri countryside. He wanted the security to provide for Rogers Jr. and the new family he was starting, and a managerial career with the Cardinals would extend his life in baseball and in his adopted hometown. But he was not yet thirty and wanted to focus still on playing.

The team he played for was not faring as well as its star. Rickey routinely made roster changes, calling up new players from the growing cache he kept on various minor league teams, but the team that seemed headed to the top of the National League a few years before had fallen to the middle of the pack. Their mediocrity, highlighted by the 65–89 record they achieved during Hornsby's record year, even compelled writer F. C. Lane to propose that the Cardinals should trade him to a better club. "His transfer," Lane wrote, "would be an undoubted benefit to the National League circuit as a whole."[29]

Breadon had no intention to do so, nor for his team to stay in the second division. When he and Hornsby encountered each other in the hotel lobby in Stockton, California during spring training, the owner had a surprising proposition for his star player: take over the manager's role from Rickey. Hornsby, for all his frustration with the current manager, insisted that Rickey was "the smartest man in baseball"; besides, he didn't want to manage at the moment anyway. Then, immediately before the season, Breadon gave Hornsby another chance to seize the reigns of the club. Once again, Hornsby declined, this time adding that "if the Good Lord himself were to come down" and take over as manager, "he couldn't do any better." The Cardinals were "a lousy team," no matter the manager.[30]

But Breadon, like Hornsby a few seasons before, was convinced of Rickey's ineptitude, especially when the team lost seven consecutive games in May to fall into last place, a position they had avoided since before Rickey became manager. He found reasons for his distaste in everything Rickey did, from his shifting line-up to his refusal to manage on Sundays. Even when Rickey traded two Cardinals benchwarmers to Chicago for Bob O'Farrell, an excellent deal for St. Louis, the owner found few kind words for the manager, acknowledging only that Rickey was more savvy with personnel decisions than strategy. Breadon watched Hornsby not only continue his consistent batting but also hit the ball even farther than ever before and decided that such skill would surely rub off on other players if Hornsby were their manager.

On May 29 at the Hotel Schenley in Pittsburgh, traveling secretary Clarence Lloyd summoned the Rajah from the lobby to Breadon's suite. Rickey met Hornsby on the way, asking his player to intervene on his behalf once again. When player and owner met, Breadon would hear no more in defense of Rickey.

"I won't have any fucking Sunday School teacher running my team!" Breadon shouted. "You're going to run it."

"No, I'm not."

"Think it over tonight and tell me tomorrow," the owner instructed. Rickey, Breadon had determined, was "through as manager" regardless of Hornsby's decision.[31] When Rickey heard the news that neither he nor his "Sunday manager" Burt Shotton would run the team, he decided that Hornsby was the best available option. Still vice president, Rickey was looking out for the franchise's best interests and convinced his second baseman to become player-manager. Tired of the hassle and admittedly curious about what he might accomplish with a team of his own, Hornsby agreed. Breadon excitedly reported the transition to the press, announcing that the Cardinals had promoted the man who might become "the greatest manager since John McGraw."[32]

Hornsby put one condition on his promotion. He wanted the chance to buy a portion of the team and have a say in its operation. Ownership would provide some protection for the future direction of his career, or so he believed, and "baseball could be my business for life."[33] Rickey, hurt by his firing but still making a tidy income on his $25,000 salary and benefits from his scouting syndicate, agreed to sell Hornsby 1,167 shares in the organization. The team's best player became its manager and one of its owners at the same time, but received no increase in salary for his added responsibility.

Hornsby's promotion rallied his team. He began by instructing his charges to forget "all that bunk this other guy has been telling you." Hornsby promised he would not "cram" the Cardinals "head(s) full of nonsense," as Rickey had, and reminded them that "It's base hits that win ball games, not smart ideas."[34] He also told them they had "only one way to go—up" and from their last place record of 13–25, they rose to one game better than .500 at season's end, good for fourth in the league.[35] Behind their manager's fiery enthusiasm for his new position and Triple Crown–winning performance at the plate, the team went 64–51 after Rickey's removal. Old wounds with fellow teammates appeared to heal as perception of Hornsby changed from a selfish and moody star to a stern but dedicated leader.

Soon after his promotion, he even physically asserted his players' rights. On a humid afternoon in St. Louis, Phillies' pitcher Jimmy Ring walked off the mound in the middle of an inning to change his sweat-soaked undershirt. Hornsby raced from the dugout to argue that Ring's break was unfair to the Cardinals and that the pitcher should finish the inning first. Philadelphia manager Art Fletcher joined the discussion at the plate, which grew into a loud argument. Suddenly, Hornsby reached back and punched Fletcher in the face, knocking the former catcher down for a few minutes and ending the discussion. Ring returned to the mound, albeit with a dry shirt obtained during the delay, and play resumed with the managers reconciled and back in their respective dugouts. After the game, reporters asked Hornsby why he'd hit Fletcher, whom Hornsby called his friend. "I couldn't make any headway against him talking," he answered.[36]

His personal statistics were as good as any season in his career. For the third time in four seasons, his batting average was over .400; at .403, he led the National League for the sixth consecutive season, another record. Also, for the second time he captured the Triple Crown, with 143 runs batted in and 39 home runs—more than Ruth and 15 more than the closest National League hitter—in a year when fewer home runs were hit than any season since 1920. Two phenomenal seasons and his promotion had also done something to alleviate Rickey's complaint that "Hornsby is a great player but he isn't the drawing card he might be."[37] The Rajah was bringing fans to Sportsman's Park and other stadiums as frequently as they had ever come.

When the season was finished, the Rajah was ready to relax. William Pennington Hornsby had been born just three days after he accepted the offer to manage, but with the demands of his new job, father had spent little time with his new son. The family planned to travel to Fort Worth to introduce Bill, as the boy was called, to his gravely ill grandmother. Then, they would move to the sod and dairy farm in Robertson, Missouri that Hornsby had acquired as an investment and off-season home, trying to enjoy a quiet winter away from the city.

Before Christmas came news the BBWAA had "correctly" named Hornsby as the league's Most Valuable Player. "If they had not done so," Arthur Mann wrote, "there would have been a riot in St. Louis, and not without reason, either."[38] Hornsby issued another humble statement but said nothing more. He was looking ahead to the next season already. One of the most famous quotes ever attributed to the Rajah probably best describes the anticipation he felt after an MVP year and before his first full season as a manager. "People ask me what I do in the winter when there's no baseball," Hornsby liked to say. "I'll tell you what I do. I stare out the window and wait for spring."[39] The season ahead would be a great one for the Cardinals and their leader.

NOTES

1. Kenneth Campbell, "Rogers Hornsby Earns Fans' Title of 'Rajah,'" *New York World*, June 5, 1927.
2. Ibid.
3. *St. Louis Post-Dispatch*, undated clipping [March, 1952], The Sporting News Archives, St. Louis.
4. Alexander, *Rogers Hornsby*, 69.
5. John P. Carmichael, *Chicago Daily News*, undated clipping [1963], The Sporting News Archives, St. Louis.
6. Jack Sher, "Rogers Hornsby: The Mighty Rajah," *Sport*, July 1949, 62–63.
7. *St. Louis Post-Dispatch*, March 16, 1922, 30.
8. Bill James, *The New Bill James Historical Baseball Abstract* (New York: Free Press, 2001), 481.
9. *Sporting News*, December 7, 1922, 1.
10. Alexander, *Rogers Hornsby*, 75.
11. George H. Williams, letter to Branch Rickey, quoted in Alexander, *Rogers Hornsby*, 75.
12. "Hornsby's Name in Divorce," *New York Times*, May 26, 1923, 5.
13. *St. Louis Post-Dispatch*, June 20, 1923, 20.
14. *St. Louis Post-Dispatch*, September 28, 1923, 37.
15. Arthur Mann, *Branch Rickey: American in Action* (Boston: Houghton Mifflin, 1957), 124.
16. John Horgan, unidentified clipping, April 14, 1973. John McGraw Archives, National Baseball Library.
17. Arthur Mann, "New York's New Babe Ruth (part 9)," *New York Evening World*, January 19, 1927.
18. *St. Louis Post-Dispatch*, February 22, 1924, 30.

19. Alexander, *Rogers Hornsby*, 87.

20. Hornsby and Surface, *My War with Baseball*, 42.

21. For most of the twentieth century, the official baseball record listed Lajoie's 1901 batting average as .422. The 1901 season was the first for the nascent American League, and statistics were not kept as accurately as they would be in later years. In the late 1990s, a reexamination of the box scores from that season found that Lajoie had actually batted .426 in 1901 and the record was corrected appropriately. Hornsby's .424 average, therefore, can now be regarded as the second-highest single-season figure in baseball's modern form, though throughout the century—and even to the present in many accounts—Hornsby was considered the record-holder. It should further be noted that in 1901, foul balls did not count as strikes under American League rules; Lajoie's .426 average, therefore, might be closer compared to nineteenth century players than to Hornsby and other hitters of the modern era.

22. The split stats cited in this paragraph come from an anonymous typewritten assessment of the season found in the Rogers Hornsby Collection at the National Baseball Library, Cooperstown, NY.

23. *Sporting News*, July 24, 1924, 5.

24. Alexander, *Rogers Hornsby*, 90.

25. J. Roy Stockton, Foreword to Hornsby, *My Kind of Baseball*, 19.

26. *Sporting News*, February 16, 1974, 30.

27. John Drebinger, "Rogers Hornsby—Star of the Cubs," *New York Times*, September 27, 1929, 35.

28. *St. Louis Post-Dispatch*, February 8, 1925, 1.

29. Franklin C. Lane, "Handicapping Baseball's Greatest Hitter," *Baseball Magazine*, March 1925, 445.

30. Hornsby and Surface, *My War with Baseball*, 42.

31. Sher, "Rogers Hornsby: The Mighty Rajah," 63; Hornsby and Surface, *My War with Baseball*, 43.

32. J. G. Taylor Spink, "The Strange Story of Rogers Hornsby," *Baseball Register* (St. Louis: The Sporting News, 1954), 3.

33. Hornsby and Surface, *My War with Baseball*, 43.

34. Drebinger, "Rogers Hornsby—Star of the Cubs," 35.

35. Hornsby and Surface, *My War with Baseball*, 43.

36. Stockton, Foreword to Hornsby, *My Kind of Baseball*, 19.

37. Lane, "Handicapping Baseball's Greatest Hitter," 445.

38. Arthur Mann, "New York's New Babe Ruth (part 10)," *New York Evening World*, January 20, 1927.

39. Hornsby's famous quote has been repeated in an almost countless number of publications. It is almost impossible to determine its original citation.

A CHAMPIONSHIP

"Yeah, when I think of baseball, I think of 1926," Les Bell, third baseman for the Cardinals, once said.[1] The year was one of many changes for the Cardinals organization and for Rogers Hornsby himself, and the batting champion's team would finally receive the accolades usually applied only to its best player. The Cardinals of 1925 were kept primarily intact for the new season and, despite the talent of McGraw's Giants and the highly regarded Pittsburgh team, the young manager expected much from his squad and told them so. To open his first spring training as a manager, Hornsby, coming off of the single greatest five-year span of hitting in the modern history of the game, brought his players together for a rare meeting. "If there's anybody in this room who doesn't think we're going to win the pennant," Hornsby instructed, "go upstairs now and get your money and go on home because we don't want you around here."[2] And though 1926 would not figure among his finest in the field or at the plate, it was a season in which Hornsby's fierce attitude as team leader would steer St. Louis to the pennant and a World Series victory over the New York Yankees—what Hornsby would describe as his "greatest moment in baseball."[3]

His first spring training would set a precedent for the way he would manage through the rest of his career. Hornsby's love of his native Texas led him to convince Sam Breadon to shift the team's training site from California back to the less accommodating Hot Wells, outside San Antonio. Miller Huggins' Cardinals had held their spring sessions in Hot Wells when the young Texan attended his first big league spring training. The place was a part of his early successes, Texas was his home, and he'd always felt that the state was perfect for baseball in

Sam Breadon (left) and family, posing with Rogers Hornsby before Game 3 of the 1926 World Series at Sportsman's Park in St. Louis. *National Baseball Hall of Fame Library, Cooperstown, N.Y.*

March. Hot Wells was not quite the resort destination that Stockton or Bradenton were, with only the underkept Terrell Hotel to accommodate the team, but it suited the no-nonsense strategies of the new manager and his spirited squad. Training opened in the dusty terrain in late February. When the Cardinals front office determined the team could stay in San Antonio and practice at the minor league Block Stadium, Hornsby put his nostalgia for Huggins' training ground aside and agreed to work his team out in the more modern environs. After just over a week in Hot Wells with his pitchers and catchers, the full organization arrived and took up residence at the Hotel Menger, near the Alamo.

Spring practice, in Rogers' opinion, was a time to focus on baseball and baseball alone. He didn't feel that players' wives should join the team for the training season, and he made an effort to minimize the team's distractions off the field. He found that the public role of a manager kept his own distractions high, however. He had always been willing to chat with a reporter in a hotel lobby or outside the clubhouse if his ideas about baseball were the topic, but he had rarely if ever sought out an audience of reporters. An audience of reporters is what he faced every day as manager, however, fielding questions on the team's progress and aspirations. He also had a long list of speaking engagements, banquets, and other public functions that as the team's star he'd managed to avoid, but as its manager found himself required to attend.

His own wife, Jeannette, joined him in San Antonio that spring, and though he may have disagreed with the idea in principle, he appreciated her presence at the time. She accompanied him to several events, and her flirty and charming manner eased the social burden for her regularly tactless husband. Rogers also took many of his steak dinners with his new friend—and horseracing bookmaker—Frank Moore. Moore and his wife came down from Kentucky to spend part of the spring at the Hotel Menger, with the Hornsbys covering the bill. Though his association with Moore must have caused some consternation for those suspicious of Hornsby's gambling habits, the bookie did allow the manager an outlet for conversation on his second favorite topic.

Horseracing, though, was a distant second, especially that spring. The player-manager was openly anxious to get his team into playing shape. Hornsby had always despised twice-daily workouts and instead instituted a longer, single practice session. The other Cardinals valued their break more than Rogers, who did not see the need for even a midday meal, and were not enthusiastic about the shift, but went along with their manager's wishes. Players on some of Hornsby's later teams would complain more vociferously about the long practice, as they would about some of Hornsby's other tendencies as manager, but Cardinals like Bell, Jim Bottomley, and Bob O'Farrell were ready to follow their fellow teammate, inspired by his managerial style that valued skill over strategy. Hornsby instructed the team that he expected the tone set at the beginning of training camp to be put to practice for the whole season. Individual players needed to constantly devote themselves to improving their performance. He was quick to let his players know that there would be no favorites on his team: a man who played hard and played well would find his way into the lineup; a Cardinal who was lazy or unproductive had "either gotta shake his habits or we'll shake him out of the league."[4]

The Texas spring was not entirely hospitable that year, with frequent thunderstorms delaying workouts and forcing exhibition games to be cancelled. Hornsby routinely convinced umpires and team management to see that games were started and finished as often as the weather would allow. He would wait out any rain delay, play through almost any weather, or, as a last resort, reschedule any game to ensure that his team would take the field. He was anxious for his team to win at every opportunity against any opponent Hornsby or Cardinals management could arrange to play in Texas; Hornsby told Breadon the team needed to acquire the "habit of winning."[5] The Cardinals had lost 118 of their final 200 games under Rickey and needed to continue the success they'd had with the Rajah as manager during the latter part of the 1925 season. Intense practice sessions were useful for straightening a hitter's stroke or tuning a pitcher's mechanics, but warming up with wins over Texas League clubs and college teams seemed vital to the team's confidence and combined performance.

The Cardinals certainly fell into the habit of winning during their Texas spring. Hornsby hit well and managed fiercely, his team running their record to 22–1 by the end of March. He learned that his mother was in failing health, and arranged to stop to see her in Austin as the team passed through. Though she was pessimistic about her own condition, she heartened them both with her confidence in the team. The St. Louis National Leaguers returned home in April to more of the rainy weather they had played through all spring and a mostly washed-out annual exhibition series with the Browns, but eager to start the regular season.

The player-manager put himself in the line-up hitting third in the only game against the Browns that wasn't rained out, and he homered before a large crowd happy to see the Hornsby-led Cards take on the junior circuit team. The Browns won the St. Louis exhibition and then started their season on the road, while the Cardinals had the privilege of hosting the first regular-season game in the renovated Sportsman's Park, which had undergone a $500,000 upgrade during the winter. Browns owner Phil Ball, at Breadon's urging, had added 9,000 seats to the stadium's capacity by adding tiers to each baseline's stands. The left-field wall was also moved back to 355 feet and right to 320, while the extremely deep center-field fence was brought forward to 420 feet by the addition of bleacher seats.[6] Not only were St. Louis fans more excited about the Cardinals chances than ever before, now more could watch them play.

Hornsby's squad, maintaining their spring roll, won five of their first six games, taking the opening series against the highly touted Pirates three to one, then tacking on two wins against Joe McCarthy's Chicago Cubs. The torrid start subsided, however, on the season's first road trip, and after losing three out of four to the Dodgers back in St. Louis over a weekend in early May—a series which Hornsby sat out with a dislocated vertebra—the team fell to 10–15. Cardinals batters started to produce bushels of runs soon enough, though, even scoring twelve or more runs three times in six games leading up to May 22, which Breadon and St. Louis mayor Victor Miller declared "Rogers Hornsby Day."

The outrage that the city and the organization had felt when Dazzy Vance rather than Hornsby was named Most Valuable Player of the 1924 season became pleasure and excitement over the Triple Crown winner's MVP award for 1925. Before the game on May 22, St. Louis took the time to recognize the player that most regarded as clearly the National League's finest player, awards notwithstanding. Mayor Miller, Breadon, Rickey, teammates, the opposing Philadelphia team, and a crowd of 14,000 heaped praise on the player-manager as he was officially awarded the medallion and canvas sack containing the 1,000 silver dollars he'd earned the season before. Hornsby was groomed for the occasion in a neatly laundered uniform with his hair carefully combed. Always confident but uncomfortable with ceremony, he smiled gratefully for the photographers, thanked all in attendance after collecting the gifts, then hustled his team out onto the field. The Cardinals dispatched the Phillies 9–2 that afternoon, with the MVP singling twice, finally evening their record at 18–18.

Despite the front office's warm praise for and clear appreciation of Hornsby's playing skills, his managing decisions, both unsuccessful and successful, were closely scrutinized. The manager resented Rickey's continued meddling with the team on the field. Aside from attempting to impose his own brand of morality on the Cardinals, Rickey was quick to provide unsolicited tips on batting stances or fielding positions, often from the owner's box in the middle of a game. Further, Hornsby refused to go along with Rickey's scheme for developing his home-grown ballplayers. The vice president brought up two of his farm system projects and encouraged the manager to work them into the pitching rotation. Hornsby felt the prospects, Bill Hallahan and Ed Clough, were too green for major league games, and declined to play them.

"But you're hindering their progress, Rog," Rickey complained.

"I'm out to win this pennant and not looking ahead to 1937," Hornsby snidely replied.

"While Clough was at Fort Smith we were offered $25,000 for him."

"If you turned that down, you're not as smart as I thought you were. He'll never pitch an important game for me."[7]

Clough never did, for Hornsby or any manager. He threw two innings and allowed five earned runs in 1926, then returned to the farm system, never to wear a major league uniform again. Hallahan did pitch sparingly and adequately in relief, then went on to an equally unexceptional ten-year career. Though it is doubtful he gave much more thought to the matter, the new manager must have taken a small pleasure in stymieing the designs of the "college-boy" ex-manager.

The St. Louis Nationals, operating enthusiastically behind the willful Hornsby, would keep their record nearly even until June 2 when they began a streak of twelve wins in thirteen games. With renewed confidence and a sense of their team's reparable deficiencies, Hornsby, Rickey, and Breadon looked toward the postseason and made two roster moves near the June 15 trading deadline that would tighten both Hornsby's lineup and his rotation, adding two players who figured decisively in the Cardinals run for the pennant.

First, Rickey made a trade with the man who had tried on several occasions to pry Hornsby himself from St. Louis, John McGraw. In a deal completed on June 14, the Cardinals and Giants swapped center fielders, Heinie Mueller to New York for Billy Southworth. The New York papers had reported for weeks that McGraw was poised to make over his line-up and that several trades were imminent. However, the usually shrewd "Little Napoleon" traded only for Mueller, and many would come to regard the move as one of McGraw's worst decisions. Southworth, whom McGraw had acquired for Casey Stengel and another player in 1924, was playing center for the Giants but was not naturally suited to the position. Though he was hitting well, his defense was seen as a liability in the Polo Grounds. Hornsby, who had Taylor Douthit to take over the middle of the outfield, put Southworth in right—which he played smoothly—and batted him fifth, to excellent results. Southworth hit .317 with 69 runs batted it and 76 scored in his ninety-nine games with the Cardinals that season. For McGraw, Mueller would hit under .250 with less than half of Southworth's runs and RBIs.

A week after the Southworth trade, the Cardinals added an experienced pitcher to their adequate but unspectacular staff, a right-hander near the end of his career who would carry the team to victory on several occasions that season, including one very significant moment that has become a part of World Series lore. On June 23, with the Cardinals in fourth place, Hornsby made a waiver claim for Grover Cleveland Alexander, one of the most successful and colorful pitchers of all time. "Old Pete," as he was widely known, had been a member of the Chicago Cubs for eight successful seasons—the Chicago fans had presented him with an automobile the same day Hornsby had been honored in St. Louis—until June 22, when, after consecutive losses and an escalating mutual irritation between the pitcher and the new Cubs manager, Joe McCarthy, he was unconditionally released.

"Alex," as Hornsby called him, was already a legend around the country. He had been among the most dominant pitchers in the National League since his career began with the Philadelphia Phillies in 1911. A three-time winner of pitching's Triple Crown (wins, strikeouts, and earned run average), by 1926 Alexander had already put several career milestones behind him, including 2,000 strikeouts and 300 wins. His career total of 373 wins ties him with Christy Mathewson for third all-time, behind Cy Young and Walter Johnson; Old Pete's 90 complete-game shutouts are second only to Johnson. Ultimately, however, he was known for his accuracy: he threw bad pitches as rarely as Hornsby swung at them. Even when intentionally throwing a ball to a batter behind in the count, Alexander would stay close to the strike zone. "I think the thing to do is to throw 'em just a little bit bad, where the hitter may be afraid to let it go by for fear the umpire will call it a strike," he once said.[8]

Alexander's personal demons were nearly as well-known as his feats on the mound, though his extended success in the face of epilepsy and alcoholism is a testament to his talents. In the middle of his career, and immediately after his third consecutive 30-win season, he was drafted into the U.S. Army during the First World War, serving an extended tour of duty as an artillery sergeant in France. He returned from the war deaf in one ear and with a severe case of shell shock; the proximity to the heavy artillery, compounding a head injury from his minor league career, also seems to have provoked the debilitating and unpredictable epileptic seizures that plagued him for the rest of his life. His epilepsy brought him sympathy, while his alcoholism—whether inspired by his war experience, his seizures, or his taste for the lifestyle—earned him a long-lasting notoriety. Rumors that he believed he pitched better with a hangover or that he spent as much game time in taverns as in the bullpen were common, and he was reprimanded and suspended for breaking training rules several times. In spite of his problems, through more than eleven major league seasons after returning from the war, extending until he was 43 years old, he won over 180 games.

By 1926, the Rajah and Old Pete had achieved a long-standing admiration for one another, each identifying the other as his greatest adversary between mound and plate. Alexander said that his Cardinals manager was the greatest batter he ever faced: "He had the greatest batting eye I ever saw. You couldn't fool him with a bad ball."[9] And at a championship-team reunion in 1936, Sid Keener quoted Hornsby telling the pitcher, "I've faced a lot of great pitchers, Grover, and I've managed a lot of great pitchers, but you're the No. 1 in my book."[10] So naturally, as Hornsby explained, he was excited by the chance to add the veteran to his staff and was pleased that the four teams below the Cardinals in the standings passed on their waiver opportunities. When Pete telephoned his former manager and current Cardinals assistant coach Bill Killefer to insist he was still in shape to pitch, Hornsby went to Breadon and convinced him to pay the $4,000 fee to acquire Alexander. Rickey, traveling at the time of the signing, might not have approved of Pete's tippling, but would come to agree that the veteran was a catalyst for the team assembled largely from his growing farm system.

It would be the most significant roster move in baseball that season. Though his fastball had lost its zip and strikeouts were fewer and farther between, the future Hall of Famer appeared in twenty-three games for Hornsby, winning nine and losing seven while his ERA was under 3.00. More significantly than his record, however, was the steady—though often hung-over—presence he brought to the Cardinals staff as he proved himself unflappable in the pressure situations of a pennant race.

Alexander, with his hair thinning, face sagging, and belt slung below his drinkers' paunch, got accustomed to his Redbirds uniform quickly, pitching a four-hitter against his former team in his debut before a jammed Sportsman's Park crowd, but the team's leader was ailing on the field. Despite respectable numbers and several timely home runs over the first half of the season, Hornsby was struggling to deal with a number of minor ailments that limited his playing time and his effectiveness. The 1925 MVP had won the Triple Crown while managing the team for the majority of the season, but many thought the responsibility of handling a club in the thick of a pennant chase may have accounted for the eighty-point drop in his average. The added tension of his mother's dissipating health may have further muddied his concentration, as he received occasional updates from the relatives caring for her in Texas, but he refused to allow that his personal distractions affected him on the field. His rationalization of his hampered individual success in 1926 was a simple and typical Hornsby explanation: "I had gotten a lot of breaks in winning 6 straight championships—averaging .400—and now a few of the breaks went the other way. It was an exciting season."[11]

Hornsby's health did affect his performance, whether he was ready to admit it or not. At the end of June, he was actually hitting well despite his pain, but with the luxury of the Cardinals steady pace of winning, he followed the team doctor's orders and had an infected carbuncle removed from his right thigh. George Toporcer, whom Tommy Thevenow had supplanted at shortstop earlier in the season, filled in at second base while Killefer took on the managing duties during the Rajah's layoff. The team lost six of nine without Hornsby, including five in a row, though he returned to managing, in street clothes, on July 5. A few days later he put himself back into the line-up, and as the team surged into a three-way race for the National League lead, the manager's contributions on the field remained minimal. His healing thigh and aching back didn't cloud his batting eye, but they surely sapped his swing of its power. Commenting on a string of walks, groundouts, and soft singles, J. Roy Stockton wrote that Hornsby "has no more in his swing than a little girl would have."[12] Frustrated by his performance, the Rajah pulled himself from the line-up once again, resting a week at the beginning of a seventeen-game road trip.

The Cardinals lost four consecutive games against the New York Giants—a team that found itself falling unusually far behind in the standings—before Hornsby put himself back in for a five-day, six-game series with the Brooklyn Dodgers that signaled the beginning of his team's championship run. The Rajah capped a sweep of the Dodgers with a game-winning double in the tenth inning on August 8, as the Cardinals commenced a remarkable streak in which they won sixteen of eighteen games. Engaged in a tight three-way battle for the National League title with Cincinnati and defending champion Pittsburgh, the St. Louis squad went 36–19 in the season's final two months.

The pennant race excited fans all over the country that season. Unlike the American League's contest, which the Yankees had dominated since May, the senior circuit provided a race in which three teams shuffled their positions as if uncomfortable to stay in one place too long. Headline writers for the sports pages drew greater attention to the standings more than to the results of individual games. On Wall Street, wagering odds were announced that reflected the unpredictability of the race. On August 26, while bets were no longer even being accepted for a Yankees A.L. pennant, odds on the streaking Cards were even, with the Pirates listed at 6 to 5 and the Reds just 8 to 5, reported the *New York Times*, "with each team receiving strong backing from its horde of adherents." Some clearly felt that the result was insignificant, however, as bettors were already placing wagers as high as $3,000 on New York to be world champs.[13]

Certainly the play of their leader and finest player spurred the Cardinals run to the pennant that season, but the Rajah was undeniably less productive than he had been before. The team as a whole, however, was generating runs and wins at a better rate than at any other time in the team's National League history. Hornsby was sparing with his compliments, but he was genuinely pleased with and outspoken about the vigorous play of his veteran teammates. In addition to Southworth, who was scoring runs almost daily since coming over from the Giants, corner infielders Bottomley and Bell were hitting exceptionally well from cleanup and fifth in the lineup, respectively. The 26-year-old Bottomley's numbers had not been far behind Hornsby's MVP stats the season before—Sunny Jim had hit .367 with 128 RBIs—and the first baseman's 1926 efforts were equally impressive at .299 and 120 RBIs. Lester Bell, never considered a great hitter, had a career year in the championship season. Reaching 100 runs batted in on the strength of a .325 batting average, Bell was the only player other than Hornsby to lead the Cardinals in OPS (on base percentage plus slugging percentage, the modern sabermetric standard for a batter's effectiveness) since the Rajah's rookie season.

Another Cardinal was enjoying the best season of his career as well, a season that the Baseball Writers of America would deem the most valuable individual performance in the National League that year. Catcher Bob O'Farrell, brought over by Rickey from the Cubs early the year before, was nearly matching his personal bests in every offensive category and was handling a pitching staff that was congealing as the season progressed. St. Louis pitchers had the third best earned run average in the National League, and were second both in strikeouts and fewest walks. As August turned to September, the staff held opponents to three or fewer runs seventeen times in nineteen games. Though his respectable offensive statistics were exceeded by the three infielders, O'Farrell's steady influence on his pitchers, his superlative defense, and team leadership led his manager to declare at the end of the season, "Bob O'Farrell was the most valuable player on my team, if such there was, and I hope he gets the most valuable player award for the league. He earned it."[14]

The manager and the owner reignited their semiregular feuding near Labor Day weekend with the team back into first and riding a winning streak. Breadon had mostly kept clear of his star player since their flare-ups during Hornsby's first season as manager and allowed Rickey, despite Hornsby's fairly open and increasing disdain for "that Ohio Wesleyan bastard,"[15] to communicate most front office matters to the clubhouse. One issue, however, Breadon took directly the clubhouse. Word had reached the owner that Hornsby had no interest in his team playing an assortment of exhibition games scheduled during September, and initially Breadon had sent word that he would call the games off. However, the owner must have felt the need for the immediate cash that gate receipts from the games would supply, or wished to assert his authority over the employee he believed was assuming too much control. The Cardinals played a doubleheader in Pittsburgh on Labor Day, winning the opener 8–1. During the break, Breadon went to the clubhouse and informed Hornsby that exhibitions in Syracuse and Buffalo were to be played en route to Boston for a weekend series. The Rajah was irate. Years later, in his autobiography, his only comment on the tight September race for the National League crown would be that his team had "almost lost the pennant" by playing the exhibitions instead of focusing on major league games and staying healthy.[16]

The Cardinals, two games ahead of the second-place Reds as they left Pittsburgh, participated in the Buffalo and Syracuse games, but Hornsby refused to play his regulars, including himself, avoiding upstate New York altogether and taking his starters to watch the American League leaders play in Yankee Stadium. The exhibitions, conspicuously without their prime attractions and marquee player-manager, hardly generated financial windfalls. Breadon, in turn, was furious, and with their team hot on the verge of a mutually desired pennant, the relationship between owner and manager was now ice cold.

The dispute may have distracted Hornsby and his charges slightly, for when the team reconvened in Boston on September 10, they were able to manage only one win in the four-game series, falling into a tie with Cincinnati. The Reds continued to play well, and a single-game season finale featuring the two pennant-hungry organizations, scheduled for the twenty-sixth, loomed. A long series against last-place Philadelphia pushed the Cardinals back on top, however. In a September 16 doubleheader, Hornsby and the Redbirds machine scored an astonishing 33 runs, and by the close of the series—having outscored the hapless Phillies 61–14 in six games—St. Louis was ahead in the race by two games.

Two games would be enough, and the season-ending showdown with Cincinnati would be meaningless in the standings. Despite having lost three of their last four, the Cardinals only needed a win against the Giants in the Polo Grounds on September 24 to clinch the pennant. Quickly down three runs on Bill Terry's first-inning homer, the team listened as Hornsby "poured acid" on them between innings. They responded with an immediate rally, tying the score and putting Toporcer on second as Southworth came to the plate, with Hornsby to follow. The right fielder remembered his manager's rasping encouragement from the on deck circle, "Have your cut, Bill. Have your cut. We need that run. It can be the pennant."[17] Southworth got a fastball from "Handsome Hughie" Mc-Quillan and lofted it into the upper tier of the Polo Grounds, lifting his new mates ahead of his old, gaining the lead that would secure the win and the National League pennant. Hornsby had asked that the Cincinnati-Philadelphia score not be displayed on the outfield board during his team's game, but after the last Giant was retired and the Reds loss posted, celebration spilled from the clubhouse to the streets of New York and to the team hotel as the Cardinals celebrated the senior circuit title; even the routinely stoic Rajah was said to take part, albeit soberly, in some pennant partying. The city of St. Louis, too, was awash with joy: the fans who'd finally turned out to Sportsman's Park in 1926 to watch the team they'd hesitantly grown to love had listened to the game against the Giants on loudspeakers throughout downtown and were rewarded with the first pennant in the organization's modern history.

In *My War with Baseball*, Hornsby would remember winning the pennant in a doubleheader against the Giants on September 28. His confusion regarding the double bill is understandable, considering the Cardinals participated in eight doubleheaders in the season's final thirty days. It is odd, and unexplainable, that he would mistake the date, however, for not only had the season ended by the twenty-eighth, but he'd also received the news the day before that he had anticipated for months: his mother, Mary Dallas Rogers Hornsby, had died.

When a practice at Yankee Stadium ended on Monday, September 27, the player-manager returned to his room to find a telegraph from his wife. She had relayed a message from his relatives at Hornsby's Bend that informed the devoted son of his mother's death. Before the season, Mary Hornsby had told her son that she was certain the Cardinals would win the pennant in 1926, and in her last days, word of the team's success had reached her. She directed her caretakers to ensure that Rogers play in the World Series. Informed of his mother's wishes, he arranged with his family to delay her funeral and remained in New York to prepare for the matchup with the Yankees "Murderers' Row."

The World Series of 1926 opened on October 2 in Yankee Stadium—in its third season, hosting the first of many World Series games—with some bookies calling the host team a 15–1 favorite to become world champions, while others, including the major New York betting commissioners, listed the teams evenly.[18] The St. Louis team certainly had less postseason experience than the Yankees, who had captured their fourth pennant in six years. Alexander, O'Farrell, Southworth, and Killefer were the only members of the entire Cardinals organization that had previously participated in a World Series. Jeannette Hornsby had traveled to New York to be with her husband after his mother died and to take in the Series, but the chance to play in front of his wife was far less exciting to the Rajah than the chance to play his first postseason games against Yankees skipper Miller Huggins, Hornsby's first major league manager. A picture of the two taken before game one shows the smiling pair shaking hands, pleased with each other's company on baseball's biggest stage.

When their charges lined up Saturday afternoon, future Hall of Famer Herb Pennock was on the mound for the Yankees and centerfielder Taylor Douthit led off for St. Louis with an opposite field shot that squeezed past Babe Ruth for a double. Southworth and Hornsby grounded out, but Bottomley managed a bloop single that pushed Douthit home for the Cardinals first and only run of the game. Southpaw Bill Sherdel started shakily in the bottom half of the first, giving up a run but not a hit, loading the bases on three walks before a

Lou Gehrig ground ball tied the score. Both teams were quiet at the plate for the remainder of Game 1: Gehrig picked up the only other RBI with a single in the sixth, and Pennock held the Cards hitless for seven innings until Bottomley singled in the top of the ninth. Bell and Chick Hafey stranded Sunny Jim at first, however, and the Yankees claimed the early series lead.

Before Game 2, Hornsby gave a pep talk, emphasizing calm and urging his players to "forget about the game being a world series' one."[19] The Cardinals reacted well. Old Pete Alexander, who was not likely to suffer from nervousness in any case, pitched masterfully, striking out ten Yankees and allowing only five to reach base in his complete game win. Hornsby collected his first hit of the series, against spitballer Urban Shocker, and continued to receive large ovations each time he came to the plate out of respect for his bereavement, according to the *New York Times*, but Southworth was the offensive star with three hits, including a 3-run home run that broke a 2–2 tie in the seventh inning.

After the 6–2 victory and a quick change to his street clothes for the trip home, Hornsby told reporters he was pleased with his team's composure behind their veteran pitcher: "The boys did everything right. They were on their toes in every play and were not the least bit nervous. I think that in the opening game some of the fellows felt the responsibility too much and it [*sic*] reacted accordingly." Crediting Alex as the root of the day's success, he said the team's collective performance was "as fine a game as I ever saw or expected."[20] After the short exchange with the press, Hornsby, the Cardinals, and a bevy of sportswriters boarded Pennsylvania Railroad's state-of-the-art train, the American, returning on the overnight trip to St. Louis for the next three games of the deadlocked series.

A frenzied crowd welcomed the National League champs back to their home city. The regular-season schedule had kept the team on the road for their final twenty-four games, and many of the players hadn't seen their wives or families since the first day of September. Likewise, the people of St. Louis hadn't seen the team for a month, either, and the scene at the railway station on Monday afternoon was frantic. Mayor Miller sent a police escort to the station, but crowds rushed to the train as it pulled to a stop, clamoring around the exits, greeting Cardinals with handshakes, backslaps, hugs, and any possible physical contact. The mayor had congratulatory bouquets for the Hornsbys and the Breadons, which barely survived into their recipients' hands. The throng pressed so close that Jeannette Hornsby, suffocated by the crowd and overcome by claustrophobia, broke into tears. A motorcade to downtown was similarly congratulated and harassed on its path, and the scarlet-clad mass that gathered in Market Square to recognize their team was described as the city's largest public assembly since Armistice Day in 1918.

The next day, St. Louis citizens gathered in record numbers again, this time with the largest crowd in the history of Sportsman's Park. In the midst of the excited clamor, Hornsby and Breadon continued their feud. A series of photos taken before the game, at the foot of the grandstand near the owner's box, show owner and manager posing together—Breadon's wife and daughters creating a wide space between the two—and flashing two of the least convincing smiles captured on film during the joyous week in St. Louis. The 37,708 fans behind them were smiling wide and yelling rabidly for the city's first postseason win, and Cardinals righthander Jesse Haines provided it. Haines had learned to throw a knuckleball the previous off-season and it had helped him to a strong 13–4 season. In Game 3, he both prevented the runs and provided them. His floating, unpredictable pitches kept the Yankee hitters off-balance for nine innings, as they managed only five hits, scoring none. Haines hustled out an infield hit in the third but was stranded by Hornsby and Bottomley. In the bottom of the fourth, the knuckleballer—who had all of one RBI during the regular season— supported his own cause by slapping a 2-run shot into the right-field bleachers, drawing gasps from the crowd and disbelieving congratulations from his teammates. The two runs were more than enough for the home team to secure the 4–0 win and the lead in the series.

If Game 3 belonged to Jesse Haines, then October 6 was indisputably Babe Ruth's day in St. Louis. The most popular player in baseball was injured and missed fifty-six games the year before, but had returned to form in 1926 and brought the Yankees back with him. His team won 91 games that season, compared to only 69 in 1925, and Ruth slugged 47 home runs with 145 runs batted in while hitting at a .372 clip. The Bronx hero only had two hits over the first three games, however, and baseball observers were anxious to see if he would break his slump in time to save the Yankees chances. Hornsby sent twenty-game winner Flint Rhem to the rubber for the second game in Sportsman's Park, but the pitcher was anything but a winner that day. In one of the greatest individual performances in World Series history, the Babe hit three awing home runs, to right field in the first inning, to right center in the third, and to dead center in the sixth. The first two he launched out of the stadium altogether. Ruth also walked twice and finished with four runs scored in Yankees pitcher Waite Hoyte's 10–5 complete game win. Hornsby had two singles and a run for his team, but struck out twice as well while he juggled his bullpen, using five pitchers in his attempt to slow Ruth.

The scoring ebbed the next day as the third record-breaking Sportsman's Park crowd in as many days saw Pennock and Sherdel each pitch ten strong innings in a tight rematch of Game 1. Sherdel took a 2–1 lead into the ninth inning, but Gehrig's "Texas-League" double to short left, followed by a bunt single by rookie Tony Lazzeri and a shot up the middle by pinch-hitter Ben Paschal, evened the score. Pennock retired the Cardinals in order to move the game to extra innings and, after Lazzeri's sacrifice fly with the bases loaded in the top of the tenth, closed out his second win of the series.

Facing what could be the final game back in Yankee Stadium, Hornsby and the Cardinals put their faith behind Grover Cleveland Alexander once again. Bottomley and Bell provided 3 runs before Alexander got to the mound in the bottom of the first, a cushion sufficient for the energized pitcher to even the Series. The Yankees were able to plate only 2 runs on their 8 hits, as Old Pete went the distance for the second time, throwing 109 pitches. The strong pitching performance coincided with the Redbirds' biggest offensive showing: ten runs, four batted in by Bell and three by Hornsby, who conferred with his star pitcher in a relieved clubhouse after the game.

The strictly sober Hornsby knew his legendary pitcher's habits and hardships and tolerated them out of respect for Pete's talents and good nature. But he reasoned with his steadiest player to keep steady for one more day. "Alex," the manager said in the visitors' locker room, "I wouldn't blame you if you felt like celebrating tonight, but don't, because if I need you I'm going to throw you right back in there tomorrow." Alexander vouched that he'd be ready the next day, saying he'd "throw four or five of the damndest balls they ever saw" on a moment's notice.[21] His actions over the next twenty-four hours are the subject of a good deal of debate and conjecture, and no single story seems more convincing than another.

Game 7 of the 1926 World Series is one of the most famous ever played, certainly the best known of all played in the first half of the twentieth century, and Grover Cleveland Alexander is at the center of the game's legend. The Sunday afternoon was dreary and drizzly, with signs that the weather might put the deciding contest on hold. New Yorkers had made a public outcry over the scarcity of tickets into the 60,000-seat stadium at the beginning of the series—even Commissioner Landis had complained—but on October 10 a mere 38,093 turned out in the dismal weather. The game got underway on time, with Haines and Hoyt facing each other again, and the Cardinals carried a 3–2 lead into the seventh, a bases loaded single by Tommy Thevenow and a Ruth solo homer the highlights of the first part of the game. Haines had a blister on his pitching hand, and though he kept the Yankees off the scoreboard, his control was suffering. After he walked Gehrig to load the bases with two outs in the bottom of the seventh, Hornsby walked in from second and examined his pitcher's bloody finger. Haines contended he could continue, but the player-manager was already determined to make a change.

The Rajah called to the bullpen for Alexander as he said he might, and the hero of Games 2 and 6 roused himself and took the field. The condition Alexander found himself in that Sunday afternoon is a subject debated in every published account of the game that arose in the years following. Most guess that the heavy drinker was undoubtedly hung-over from a night of celebration. Flint Rhem, who was in the left-field pen with Alexander during the game and served as one of his drinking companions that season, claimed Pete had spent the first six and a half innings sleeping on a bench with a pint of whiskey in his sweater pocket. Alexander would maintain until his death that he'd abstained the previous night. An article by Commissioner Ford Frick in 1961 says the legend of Pete's hangover is false, that he was alert and had watched every play of the game and had decided to warm up as Haines struggled. Hornsby later said, "Hell, I'd rather have [Alexander] pitch a crucial game for me drunk than anyone I've ever known sober. He was that good."[22] But he was unsure of the pitcher's condition, so he met his friend on the way to the mound to be sure he was ready. "I wanted to look at his eyes," he would explain afterwards. They were clear.[23]

Frick's account aside, Alexander barely warmed up—he rarely did—but he took his time before pitching. The rookie Lazzeri waited, tapping dirt from his cleats, as the pitching change slowly developed. Alexander took the mound and, seeing there was no place for Lazzeri on the loaded bases, told his catcher O'Farrell, "I guess I'll just have to give him nothin' but a lot of hell."[24] He straightened his undersized cap; Lazzeri waited. He adjusted his belt; Lazzeri waited. He kicked at the rubber, looked around the bases, and finally delivered his first pitch: inside for a ball. The next pitch, a second fastball, was inside as well, but caught the corner for a called strike. Pete's third pitch was a fastball on the inside again—off the plate according the O'Farrell—and Lazzeri made contact, rocketing the ball deep toward the left-field stands, deep enough for a grand slam, but foul by a few yards. Alexander paused as the stadium's swell subsided after the long drive, then delivered two breaking balls toward the outside. Lazzeri waved unsuccessfully at each. The inning was over, and Alexander's World Series legend was born.

The game didn't end there, though many of the Alexander myths mistake that seventh inning for the ninth. Alexander pitched two more frames, getting the first six hitters he faced (including Lazzeri) out in order. With two outs in the bottom of the ninth, Babe Ruth approached the plate. Alexander was no fool: though he took Ruth to a full count, he kept his pitches off the plate and let Ruth have first on balls. (The walk was Ruth's 11th of the series, a major league record that would stand until Gene Tenace of the Oakland Athletics tied it in 1973 and San Francisco Giant Barry Bonds broke it in 2002 with 13.) The next hitter was Bob Meusel, with Lou Gehrig on deck. Ruth saw an opportunity to put himself in scoring position and took off for second on Alexander's first pitch to Meusel. Alexander's memory of the moment illustrates it best: "I caught the blur of Ruth starting for second as I pitched and then came the whistle of the ball as O'Farrell rifled it to second. I wheeled around and there was one of the grandest sights in my life. Hornsby, his foot anchored on the bag and his gloved hand outstretched, was waiting for Ruth to come in. There was the Series and my second big thrill of the day."[25]

In every interview Hornsby granted from October 11 until his death almost forty years later, he made a consistent answer to the question of which of his accomplishments he was most proud. Tagging Ruth out at second to end the 1926 World Series was his reply each time; he called the play was "my biggest thrill" and the "biggest surprise of my career."[26] For all of his individual success and well-reported arrogance, the player-manager was interested in his team's success above all else. He never diminished his own role in their success, but like any great player, a team championship was the achievement he desired most. Though he began each season with the hope that another title awaited him at the end, 1926 would be the only time in his long baseball career that he was part of a world championship team.

The Cardinals returned by train to St. Louis and another rowdy welcoming committee on October 11. Most of the other players celebrated for days, gathered with Mayor Miller, Missouri governor Sam Aaron Baker, and fans from across the state in Sportsman's Park, attended banquets, and cashed their winners' checks for $5,585.51 apiece that arrived quickly from Commissioner Landis. Meanwhile, Rogers, Jeannette, and Billy Hornsby were on their way to Austin. With his duties to his championship team resolved, Hornsby's attention returned to the memory of his late mother. He issued a statement to the people of St. Louis via wire from New York, asking that they celebrate with his players and excuse him in his grief.

At his aunt's home in Austin, four generations of the Hornsby and Rogers family assembled to remember Mary. The St. Louis organization sent a large bouquet of bright red roses that rested on her casket. At the ceremony, tears streamed down Rogers' face as a minister read a letter written by Mary's infirm brother, Professor J. B. Rogers. The letter recounted Mary's happy demeanor and pleasure that she lived her last years "with her heart bursting with pride in the achievements of her baby."[27] The family then rode in a procession of black cars nine miles out to the cemetery at Hornsby's Bend, where her body was laid to rest beside her husband who had died twenty-five years before. It was not until after her interment that many of his relatives finally circled around Rogers to congratulate him on the Cardinals success and, in the case of many second and third cousins, to meet the baseball hero for the first time.

Back in Texas where his championship team had initiated their winning habits that spring, the player who had now accomplished nearly every goal a hitter or a manager could conceive had a chance to reflect on the season and on his twelve-year major league career. Despite his beloved mother's passing, he was undoubtedly very happy with the position of his career and his life. As he and his young family boarded a train to return to Missouri, Hornsby was assessing not the quality of that career, but the value he put on it. Even World Series victors conduct business in the off-season; the Cardinals and their player-manager would have a good deal to attend to in the coming months.

NOTES

1. Golenbock, *The Spirit of St. Louis: A History of the St. Louis Cardinals and Browns*, 100.

2. Ibid.

3. *Chicago Daily-News*, March 1, 1943, 22.

4. *St. Louis Post-Dispatch*, March 21, 1926, 26.

5. Alexander, *Rogers Hornsby*, 109.

6. Curt Smith, *Storied Stadiums: Baseball's History Through Its Ballparks* (New York: Carroll & Graf, 2001), 132.

7. Thomas Holmes, "Rickey, Flat Failure as Manager, Is Power Behind St. Louis Team," clipping, February 1931, Branch Rickey Collection, The Sporting News Archives, St. Louis.

8. "Hornsby Greatest Batter He Ever Faced, Alexander Says, Recalling His 20-Year Career," clipping, [1931], Grover Cleveland Alexander Collection, National Baseball Library, Cooperstown, NY.

9. Ibid.

10. Sid Keener, *St. Louis Post-Dispatch* [July 1916], Grover Cleveland Alexander Collection, National Baseball Library, Cooperstown, NY.

11. Hornsby and Surface, *My War with Baseball*, 44.

12. *St. Louis Post-Dispatch*, September 14, 1926, 32.

13. "Cards Even, Pirates Six to Five to Win Flag," *New York Times*, August 27, 1926, 13.

14. *Sporting News*, September 30, 1926, 2.

15. Alexander, *Rogers Hornsby*, 114.

16. Hornsby and Surface, *My War with Baseball*, 44.

17. Golenbock, *The Spirit of St. Louis: A History of the St. Louis Cardinals and Browns*, 107.

18. James R. Harrison, "Yanks Have Shade on the Cardinals," *New York Times*, October 1, 1926, 17.

19. "Hornsby is Pleased by Change in Team," *New York Times*, October 4, 1926, 27.

20. Ibid.

21. *Sporting News*, November 15, 1950, clipping, Grover Cleveland Alexander Collection, National Baseball Library, Cooperstown, NY.

22. Hornsby and Surface, *My War with Baseball*, 193.

23. Ford Frick and Frank Graham, "Baseball's Greatest Dramas: Alex Fans Lazzeri," *New York Journal-American*, March 21, 1961, 31.

24. *Sporting News*, November 15, 1950.

25. Quoted in Golenbock, *The Spirit of St. Louis: A History of the St. Louis Cardinals and Browns*, 117.

26. Hornsby and Surface, *My War with Baseball*, 192.

27. "Hornsby Bowed in Sorrow as Mother Is Laid to Rest," clipping, October 14, 1926, Rogers Hornsby Collection, National Baseball Library, Cooperstown, NY.

"NEW YORK'S NEW BABE RUTH"

The confetti from the championship celebrations had barely been swept out of the street before Hornsby's Cardinals career would end abruptly. Still working under a three-year contract negotiated before he was named manager in 1925, Hornsby was due to earn $30,000 in 1927. With his playing record now undisputable and his managerial success at its pinnacle, Hornsby sat down with Sam Breadon to negotiate a new agreement which he felt fairly accounted for his dual achievements. Their meeting was brief, and Hornsby left bound to the Cardinals by the same contract. Within two days, however, the biggest star of the National League and the third year of that contract were the property of the New York Giants.

After their dispute over the September exhibition games, Breadon and his manager had spoken very little during the final days of the 1926 season—even in the aftermath of the world championship—and their contract discussion on December 20 healed no wounds. The Rajah, despite holding three valuable real estate properties in and around St. Louis, earning one of the largest salaries in baseball, and having been in negotiations for a Hollywood film pact reported at $200,000, believed he needed a new contract with the Cardinals, not just as a fiscal reward for what he had earned the team, but as acknowledgement of his importance to the entire organization. In this fifteen-minute conference, Breadon offered to replace Hornsby's $30,000 deal with a one-year contract for $50,000—a sum that would be the highest salary ever paid a player or manager in the history of the National League. Hornsby refused, claiming that he'd earned not just the raise but a commitment from the team for three more years at that rate. Breadon silently stood his ground for the rest of the meeting as Hornsby defended his demands and, according to some reports, insisted that the owner's choices were to sign him to a three-year contract or to trade him.

If Hornsby did demand a trade, it likely only set in motion a plan that the owner had established well before entering contract negotiations. Beginning immediately after the Series, rumors had been circulating that not only was Hornsby at odds with Breadon over team issues, but that the Giants were actively pursuing him. In October, the *Sporting News* passed on rumors of the possible trade and opined that "it would prove the death knell of the St. Louis National League team, now riding on the top of popularity, if such a move were even to be considered."[1]

Though Breadon and Branch Rickey had rebuffed offers from the Giants for years, Stoneham and McGraw never wavered in their interest in the Cardinals star. Time and time again in talks over Hornsby, Frankie Frisch had been the one player with whom McGraw refused to part, but there had been a falling out between McGraw and Frisch during the season as well. When Rickey had approached McGraw with the possibility of trading Hornsby at the league meetings in early December, the Giants coach implied that he'd be willing to give up the "Fordham Flash."

Despite their personal differences with Hornsby, Rickey and Breadon would not have shipped their star player and manager off to New York without some provocation—they knew the record attendance at Sportsman's Park in 1926 was not attributable to Lester Bell's hitting or Tommy Thevenow's glove work—but a contract dispute offered an opportunity to reestablish their authority over a team they felt Hornsby had seized as his own. Following the failed negotiations, Breadon acted quickly, following through within two days on a proposal likely made even before he talked with Hornsby. Beginning nearly the minute his manager walked out of his office, Breadon began placing calls to Giant's owner Charles Stoneham, seeking him out at home, at his office, through his assistants, almost eager to tell him, "you've got Hornsby." The two owners worked out a deal quickly—Stoneham did not even consult McGraw, who'd had a hand in every roster move for over two decades—and went straight to the press to reveal the trade that would be described as the most significant of the young twentieth century. Saying that Hornsby left "no alternative for us," Breadon and the Cardinals announced on December 22, 1926 that the team's player-manager had been dealt to the New York Giants for second baseman Frisch and pitcher Jimmy Ring.[2]

To the press, Breadon tried to stave off accusations that he'd submarined his club's fortunes by trading its star. He insisted that Hornsby provoked the trade and couched the event in terms of a power-grab by the arrogant player-manager.

"Hornsby did remarkably well with the Cardinals last season, but there are some things a club can't stand for—and that is the manager trying to dictate to the club," Breadon said in defense of his action.[3] Hornsby issued a statement that explained his position on the contract dispute and expressed feeling for the fans who had supported him though his whole career. Through the rest of his career he would always describe the trade, which came less than two months after his "biggest thrill in all baseball," as "the biggest disappointment I had in my life."[4]

The furor that surrounded even the idea of trading Hornsby extended into the commentary on the deal's details. Jimmy Ring was regarded as a mediocre but consistent pitcher and Frisch, despite an uninspiring 1926 season in which he hit .314 with only 5 home runs and 44 RBIs, was thought to be a future star player in his own right, but many thought the trade especially lopsided, particularly when Breadon announced that no cash had been involved in the transaction. Several accounts claim that anywhere between $25,000 and $100,000 went from New York to St. Louis with Frisch and Ring, but various others verify the official listing of the trade, which notes only the two-players-for-one swap. Breadon claimed that he could not justify a commitment of $150,000 to his star player, but trading him away for apparently so little seemed to Cardinals observers to be bad business as well.

St. Louis fans, unimpressed by Breadon's public rationalizations, were outraged about the deal that sent the city's biggest sports hero of the last decade away in the blink of an eye. Some columnists at the *Post-Dispatch* and the *Sporting News* may have agreed with the owner's impressions of Hornsby as self-centered, arrogant, and ungrateful, but few would have dared to claim he was a detriment to the team or the organization. Others were brutally critical of Breadon and his "henchman" Rickey. One sportswriter promised a permanent boycott of the Cardinals, insisting that the Browns were now the only major league team playing in Sportsman's Park. Another group of writers and fans petitioned Commissioner Landis to overturn the deal altogether. They managed no formal effect, but the city's clear disapproval was registered and placed a unique pressure on Breadon, Frisch, and the team's new manager to defend the world championship.

Breadon had approached Bill Killefer about taking over the managerial post even before the trade was complete, but out of loyalty to his friend Hornsby, Bill refused the position. Without Killefer to take the job, the Cardinals had no one in the organization with coaching experience aside from Rickey, who neither wanted nor was offered the chance to return to the field. So, again, the owner assigned one of his own players to a hyphenated post. "What a position to be in, huh?" asked Bob O'Farrell, looking back on his abrupt promotion from MVP catcher to player-manager. "Hornsby couldn't get along with the owner . . . and in a way I end up as the goat. I didn't want to be the manager. I was in the prime of my career, only thirty years old, and managing always takes something away from your playing."[5] Like Hornsby, the stout catcher's teammates already admired his leadership before he took over as their manager, and though he didn't possess the Rajah's brisk, brusque, and efficient manner, he was similarly hands-off in style and had a successful year. He would only be the third manager in Breadon's remarkable span of owner interference between 1925 and 1929. The Cardinals boss would set a precedent not even the notorious George Steinbrenner ever succeeded in matching: He changed managers five times within those five seasons, even naming Billy Southworth to the head job twice.

The city of New York welcomed Hornsby with as much passion as St. Louis spent trying to keep him. A nine-day series in the *New York Evening World* by master sportswriter Arthur Mann heralded the new Giant as "New York's New Babe Ruth." Though praising a player by equating him with a contemporary may seem an odd way to declare a star, the comparison with the most popular player in baseball's history gave an indication of what New Yorkers expected from the city's newest sport celebrity. Coming off a disappointing 1926 campaign, the Giants and their fans were anxious to return to the annual pennant races. Hornsby, entering his twelfth major league season, was still the most respected hitter in the senior circuit, and his recent success as manager gave hope to New York's followers who were unsure what the future after McGraw's tenure as manager would hold for their team. Now, concerns that McGraw's inconsistent health meant his imminent retirement turned to hope that he had hand-picked a successor who would continue his legacy of greatness. Hornsby's acquisition indicated that the team's future had been stabilized, but critics did wonder aloud if Stoneham had brought that future to McGraw sooner than he wanted.

The Rajah was delighted with the chance to play for the 55-year-old McGraw, "the greatest manager in the world" who handled baseball business, on and off the field, "the way I like to do it—yes or no, without any hagglin' or moanin'— no small town stuff."[6] He went to New York at the beginning of the new year to meet with his manager and to negotiate a contract. McGraw and Stoneham agreed to replace the final year of Hornsby's St. Louis contract with a two-year pact worth between $36,000 and $40,000 per year. He was also appointed as Giants team captain, an honor Frisch had carried the previous season—unreliably, in McGraw's view. So "New York's New Babe Ruth" made arrangements to investigate moving his family to the city and to resolve his financial affairs in St. Louis. Some parts of the transition would happen easily and profitably, while others would cause headaches for Hornsby, his new and former owners, and a small host of others around St. Louis and the National League.

The first and easiest matter was selling his downtown apartment buildings. It was a prosperous time in St. Louis as in the rest of the country, and investors quickly purchased his property, earning Hornsby a modest profit. He kept his rural Missouri farm, intending to use it as a permanent off-season home, but did not have a clear plan for his living arrangements during the season, or for how Jeannette and Billy would live during his season in New York. It appeared that he would live in a Manhattan hotel while his wife and son stayed at the home in Missouri.

Not inclined as a manager to rely heavily on paperwork, he had little to remove from his small Sportsman's Park office. But the paper that tied him to the Cardinals was not kept in the clubhouse anyway: Hornsby still owned 1,167 shares in the team. National League President John Heydler had privately ruled that Hornsby could not play for the Giants as long as he owned a piece of the Cardinals. St. Louis stockholders complicated matters further on January 31, when, at the annual directors' meeting, they declared a 10 percent dividend payment on the championship year's earnings (netting Hornsby an extra $2,916) and voted their rival's new team captain back to his position on the board. Breadon was angry, but saw the muddle as an opportunity to regain shares of a newly profitable stock; Heydler was flustered and reiterated his stance that he could not allow Hornsby to play for one team and own part of another.[7]

Rogers was willing to sell, but did not rush to part with his stock on anyone's terms but his own. He had the stock appraised by a New York professional, who valued it at $150 per share. Acknowledging that he would never get the appraised value for his large holdings, he told reporters that he knew Breadon was refusing offers of $135 per share for his own controlling interest in the club. Hornsby had paid Rickey less than $43 per share in 1925 and now, less than eighteen months later, he announced what he believed to be a fair asking price of $105 per share to Breadon and the other Cardinals shareholders. The owner refused the price and there was little more discussion at that moment, though the team started to cast about for a prospective buyer. Hornsby retained his attorney William Fahey to control negotiations as he set off with Jeannette and Billy for Sarasota, Florida, home of Giants spring training camp.

The matter proceeded quietly during February and early March, as Fahey maintained the upper hand in any talks: the Cardinals stock was his client's to hold or sell as he pleased, while the contract with the Giants was likewise guaranteed. Breadon insisted that Hornsby sell, Stoneham insisted that Hornsby sell, and McGraw insisted that Hornsby sell; their urgency only made it easier for Fahey to demand Hornsby's price. Heydler was at the root of the turmoil, as he had the responsibility of pacifying the two teams with primary interests in the situation as well as six other teams concerned with the conflict of interest and a bona fide superstar the fans would demand to see play. Arriving in Florida a week before he was required, the Rajah, unperturbed as usual by business matters once he stepped into the batter's box, took up his new team's training regimen with a body healed and rested from the acquired ailments of the year before. His weight was back up, his back was strong, and the freedom from managerial responsibility gave him much more time in the batting cage to warm up his swing.

He also had more time to spend with his family. During 1926 spring training, Billy had stayed in Missouri under the care of his nurse, but in Florida with his parents in 1927, the toddler was able to lure his father away from evenings in the hotel lobby. His son was also able to provide a distraction from troubles lingering over Hornsby's spring training companion of 1926, the bookmaker Frank Moore. Less than a year after the Hornsbys had hosted the Moores at the Hotel Menger in San Antonio, the bookie had filed a suit against the ballplayer that alleged that Hornsby owed him over $70,000 in unpaid gambling debts and personal loans. Moore had begun his litigation in mid-January, but by the beginning of spring training, preliminary proceedings in the St. Louis city courts had led only to a postponement of the trial until after the baseball season, and Hornsby's statement that he didn't owe Moore so much as a dime. The headache of a trial would be delayed, but the public facts of the case would amplify the attention the commissioner's office and New York ownership had already focused on Hornsby's increasingly notorious gambling habits. Hornsby himself wanted only to gamble and to play baseball, separately and in peace.

In his first game wearing a Giants uniform, Hornsby played much like he had in a Cardinals jersey. Helping his team to a 13–1 win over the Browns, he turned a pair of double plays and rapped three hits on a cool Florida afternoon in early March. During the exhibition season, Hornsby would play like his younger self—and demand that his new teammates press themselves into midseason form as well. As player-manager of the Cardinals, Hornsby rightfully expected his teammates to obey his instructions and absorb his suggestions, but his blunt criticisms often inspired only ire from his fellow Giants. However, with McGraw away from camp for reasons varying from a drinking and gambling visit to Havana to a contract negotiation with new outfielder Edd Roush in late March, the team captain was effectively the manager, leading practices and running exhibition games.

He occasionally rankled his teammates in that role. At one practice where McGraw left Hornsby in charge, the team was working on double plays. When Hornsby gave instructions to third baseman Lindstrom, Freddie protested, "But the Old Man always told me differently." The Rajah cut him off, and said, "McGraw's sick and I'm running this ball club. You do it my way now." Lindstrom turned away in disgust. "You and your ideas," he muttered. "Once you lay aside your bat, you're a detriment to any ball club."[8]

Not everyone felt Hornsby's leadership would hurt the team. The combined effort of the Rajah and Little Napoleon was newsworthy heading into the regular season. Richard Vidmer wrote in the *New York Times* that McGraw was "anxious" to apply the theory "about two heads being better than one" to managing. Vidmer revealed McGraw's plan to accommodate the talents of two championship-caliber managers: "All the thinking that requires deep meditation and concentrated brain power will be done by McGraw; the snap judgment or short dashes will be left to Hornsby." What exactly fell under each category of thinking was left vague, other than that the second baseman would be responsible for "adjustments" on the field that McGraw would not be able to "leave the bench and go see to." Vidmer concluded that though the manager was not yet ready to retire, it didn't "take a cross-word puzzle dictionary to figure out who will be McGraw's successor."[9]

Vidmer also got McGraw on the record regarding Frank Frisch's shortcomings as team captain, contributing an insider's perspective on the topic that the New York and St. Louis papers watched intently throughout the spring. Comparisons of Hornsby and Frisch were daily news material, and McGraw's comments on his former player showed how ready he had been to replace his budding star with the established one. "I've always tried to get my captains to help out with running the club," he said. "Frisch used to think his day's work was over when he handed the umpire the batting order. If I wanted to call his attention to something during the game, he generally was looking for his cap or a bird flying around or anything except the bench."[10]

The parallel reports from Avon Park, Florida, where the Cardinals made their spring headquarters in 1927, were that the defending champs were a "better ball club than last year." Hornsby issued a measured estimation of his former team in the same breath as a prediction for a Giants pennant: "The Cardinals won't have the same spirit they had last year." He declined to comment on the reason why. Breadon, still trying to quell the fury he provoked by trading Hornsby, boldly proclaimed that Frisch was "a better defensive player, a better base runner and he won't hit any worse than Rogers did last year" ("with emphasis, of course, on the last year," Vidmer added).[11] The statistical comparison of the two second basemen favored Hornsby at the end of spring training. The *Times* ran a separate item on March 31 to point out that Frisch had hit .379 and scored three runs for the Cardinals in Florida, while the new Giant batted .407 and scored 12 times.[12]

As the team boarded trains to return to New York, the Giants faced the possibility that both their middle infielders would be on the sidelines when the season opened in the Philadelphia Baker Bowl against the Phillies. Standout short-stop Travis Jackson had emergency surgery for appendicitis on April 1, and his doctors estimated that he would be out of action for at least six weeks. On the other hand, John Heydler was calling for an emergency meeting to separate Hornsby from his Cardinals stock. While he was privately summoning Hornsby, his lawyer Fahey, and the eight National League owners to negotia-tions in Pittsburgh, he was also insisting to the press that Hornsby would never take the field as a Giants player and a Cardinals owner. On April 3, using a muddled logic defended by the "unwritten laws of baseball," Heydler told re-porters, "No, I cannot suspend Hornsby for his owning St. Louis National League club stock and playing with the New York National League club. But I can prevent him from playing while he does own the stock." Pressed to say if he would follow through, he said "I would rather cross that bridge when I come to it."[13]

On April 6, Heydler called Hornsby at the Richmond Hotel in Augusta, Georgia to encourage him to resolve the matter quickly, before the affair esca-lated into a perpetual legal battle. A lawyer in New York had warned the Na-tional League president that an injunction would be filed on Hornsby's behalf to keep him on the field, and Heydler assured the player that he and the Na-tional League had hired counsel and would fight in court. "That won't get us anywhere or baseball anywhere," Heydler said. Hornsby's unfailing response to every proposal Heydler presented was "wish you'd get in touch with Mr. Fahey," or "Fahey knows all about it—more than I do."[14]

To reporter Frank Graham, Hornsby did lay out the three resolutions he found acceptable. The first was that Breadon and the Cardinals organization would trade ownership of their Houston franchise in the Texas League for his St. Louis shares, an approximately equal exchange. "I'll trade my stock for that in a second," the native Texan declared. Second would be that the Giants cover the difference between an $80 per share offer from an investor named Pritchard and Hornsby's asking price—though Hornsby would admit to Heydler and oth-ers that he thought Pritchard was a "fly-by-night." The third option Hornsby proposed was that all eight National League teams pool together and buy his shares at the $105 price and hold the stock to sell at the best opportunity.[15]

The minor league Houston team might have been most attractive to Hornsby, but a combination of the latter options was closer to what he received. The ballplayer and representatives for the owners convened in Pittsburgh on April 8. At the William Penn Hotel, Hornsby and Fahey lounged in their rooms and in the massive art deco lobby while the owners hashed out possible solutions to the problem. Shuttling from the owners' meeting room to Hornsby and back through much of the night, Giants attorney Leo Bondy kept negotiations moving forward. Breadon refused to rise above his offer of $85, while Hornsby stuck to his price. Their persistence paid off for both, as Heydler's urgency and the other teams' growing impatience forced a deal which paid Hornsby $116,700 for his 1167 shares. The sum would be divided with New York paying $17,500, the other National League teams contributing a combined $17,500, and Breadon suddenly paying only $70 per share for complete control of Hornsby's holdings.

Heydler quickly sent a wire to Commissioner Landis: "Hornsby stock dispute settled today by the payment of one hundred per share for the stock which will now revert to Mr. Breadon STOP A high price to pay for a principle but I believe it will all redown [*sic*] to the best interest of the game."[16] The principle Heydler paid for can be considered the root of most of the modern conflict-of-interest rules written into collective bargaining agreements and league by-laws of the major sports league. The case would be routinely referenced in similar circumstances many years after Hornsby held no stake in any club.

The large transaction was scheduled to take place on or before April 15, and Heydler officially cleared Hornsby to play. Edd Rousch had not joined the team until their northward trek, but he was quickly readying himself and proved to McGraw that he would hit well in the line-up's third spot. This meant that Hornsby, who had hit third for most of his career, would be the cleanup hitter in a Giant's lineup that had scored more than 10 runs in several preseason contests. They scored 19 runs in the final exhibition game of the spring, an annual meeting with the U.S. Military Academy team at West Point, New York. In the season opener at Philadelphia, with Heydler on hand to watch his recent nemesis, the Giants continued to score runs with ease. In the first regular-season game of his career in which he didn't wear a Cardinals uniform, Hornsby homered as he and his new teammates posted 15 runs to beat the Phillies.

McGraw's squad finished April in first place and, on the strength of their impressive offense, pushed their record to 19–9 by mid-May. The health of the Giants skipper was unsteady, as the allergies he suffered annually were compounded by his increasing age; by the end of May, he had turned over day-to-day operation of the club to his team captain. Under Hornsby, the offense continued to thrive, but the pitching declined as quickly as McGraw's health had. To bolster the defense, he quickly reinstated Travis Jackson as the other half of his double-play combination, benching Doc Farrell, the University of Pennsylvania graduate who was hitting as well as any of his mates in the potent line-up, but whom Hornsby thought to be incapable in the field. As Hornsby biographer Charles Alexander points out, Jackson's return from his appendectomy created a unique occurrence in baseball's history. The entire infield—Bill Terry at first, Hornsby at second, Fred Lindstrom at third, and Jackson at short—would all end up enshrined at Cooperstown.[17]

A Hall of Fame infield couldn't keep the ball in the park, though, as Giants pitchers surrendered runs at a rate their teammates could not match. Their poor pitching eventually dropped their record to .500 and they collapsed to fourth in the National League, a spot they would hold steadily for the better part of three months. Their May misfortunes continued even when McGraw returned to the dugout in early June, on the Giants first trip to St. Louis that season. The New Yorkers arrived in the evening on June 14 with a five-game losing streak in tow, but their record was not nearly as interesting to Cardinals fans as their second baseman. Hornsby was welcomed back like a triumphant general, albeit without his army, in his first major public appearance in the city since he had led their team to the championship. The Giants train was met at Union Station by a horde of fans in a scaled repetition of when Hornsby and the Redbirds arrived for Game 3 of the World Series the year before. The novelty drew large crowds to Sportman's Park on Wednesday and Thursday afternoon. After Jesse Haines shut them out in the series' first game, the Giants finally broke their losing streak and their offensive slump, winning the second 10–5 behind a 2-run homer by Hornsby.

Breadon, either out of deference to Hornsby's undeniable part of the championship season or to put Hornsby's separation from his former teammates on display, chose the game on Saturday to raise the pennant flag for 1926 and distribute World Series' rings. A near-sellout crowd, including Mayor Miller and U.S. Secretary of War Dwight Davis, turned out for Charles Lindbergh Day. The *Spirit of St. Louis* pilot and Judge Landis handed the members of the championship team their rings, beginning with Hornsby in his gray flannels, then on to Bob O'Farrell, Pete Alexander, and their teammates; tributes from Miller and others thankfully kept analogies between the '26 champs and Lindbergh's plane to a minimum. Alexander—who at 40 years old and drinking more than ever managed to pitch 22 complete games en route to a 21–10 record in 1927, his finest season since 1920—was O'Farrell's starter that day. Old Pete allowed a double to his friend Hornsby and was not at his best, but he earned a 6–4 win with the help of Jim Bottomley's 3-run home run.

Being back in St. Louis also gave Hornsby an opportunity to spend time with his wife and growing son, whom he saw sparingly during his season with the Giants. In Manhattan, he lived in a series of small bachelor's apartments; his personal habits did not require lavish accommodations and, considering Billy's age and the National League schedule, Jeannette and the boy did not travel to the east coast that year. Rather than have his family stay on the farm, Hornsby rented rooms at the Forest Park Hotel in St. Louis, the town his wife still considered their home, with the intention of making a permanent off-season home in Robertson and securing a more suitable New York apartment for the family before the next season.

The National League star was firmly fixed in New York by midseason. Hornsby was hitting well, back at or near the top of the leagues statistics—though his batting average did trail that of his new "rival" Frisch and the eventual winner of the batting title, young Pittsburgh outfielder Paul Waner. Batting cleanup gave the Rajah more runners on base ahead of him, while the bats of Terry and Jackson following him assured that he would see lots of pitches in the strike zone. Even so, Hornsby walked 87 times that season, most in the National League. His always consistent batting eye meant that, true to his old form, pitches were either out of the zone or struck hard for hits.

The managerial transition from McGraw to Hornsby also appeared imminent. On July 19, the Giants hosted a silver jubilee celebration for the Little Napoleon before a game against the Cubs. Stoneham, Hornsby, and a host of others from around the city and the league paid tribute to twenty-five years of Giants baseball under the command of their stout, stocky manager. Honored by several speeches and a large crowd, McGraw received a giant silver cup and greeted a number of his former players. In his quarter century with the New York club, McGraw had led his charges to ten pennants and three world championships. In 1927, he was clearly tiring to all observers, and Hornsby, who managed more than a third of the team's games that year, seemed ready to step in. Though both denied it publicly, the whole of New York believed it was an inevitable change.

In June, just days before the games in St. Louis, an article had appeared in the *New York Herald-Tribune* under the headline "McGraw to Quit, Hornsby to Get Job, West Hears." Typically, McGraw was flattering in his praise of the Rajah, and had been for several years; the *Herald-Tribune* article, however, quoted the Giants manager heaping lavish praise on his second baseman. McGraw reportedly said he was "getting tired of traveling" and that he planned to "step out as manager" shortly. The report went on to quote McGraw saying "Hornsby is the man to carry on. The members of the club all swear by Hornsby. He has proved the greatest inspiration a team could desire, and he has more than fulfilled all expectations we had in signing him." A correction printed on June 16 tempered the McGraw quotes and noted that McGraw had in fact said "that when he did retire Hornsby would in all probability succeed him." McGraw added that in any event, Stoneham and the Giants board of directors ultimately would choose the next manager.[18]

From his experiences with Breadon, Hornsby clearly knew the role that ownership would play in the future of his career. He never spoke with reporters about his "imminent" promotion other than to reiterate that he intended to play with the Giants as long as he was welcome. Whether Hornsby or McGraw would manage the team in 1928 was left to silent speculation from that point forward, but during 1927, Hornsby did manage the team consistently in McGraw's absence. His efforts in the early part of the season had had negligible effect, but when McGraw again felt ill enough to release control of the team again, the Giants began to win. Hornsby's impact as manager is debatable—several teammates grumbled at his idiosyncratic approach to the role—but the team's success while he was manager is not. Though they bristled at Hornsby's increased demands that they "improve" their personal habits, such as curtailing their drinking and increasing their sleeping, the Giants record was 42–16 from the day McGraw asked Hornsby to lead the team out on a road trip beginning July 27 until the end of the season. The official record lists Hornsby as manager for thirty-two games in 1927, with a record of 22–10, but he was in charge of day-to-day strategy for the better part of the season's stretch run.

Hornsby's contributions as manager may be difficult to assess, but on the field, he was the key weapon in a consistent offensive attack. Terry, Jackson, Lindstrom, Roush, and George Harper were all playing at their best by August (each would finish with a batting average over .300), and younger McGraw projects were providing needed depth. Eighteen-year-old Mel Ott, for example, in his second season of part-time play, hit an inside-the-park home run at Wrigley Field in the first game of Hornsby's second-half stint as manager, and would provide a needed rest for Roush and other outfielders on occasion for the rest of the season. (The home run was the first of Ott's Hall of Fame career; it would also be his only inside-the-park home run, though he would hit 510 of the more common variety.)

Hornsby himself was as fearsome at the plate as he had ever been. His batting average, which had hovered around .330 for a good part of the season, shot up to near .360 by season's end. His home run total, kept low in New York by the Polo Grounds' unique shape, continued to grow while the team was on the road; his 133 runs led the National League. *New York Times* sportswriter James Harrison dismissed the idea that Hornsby's new responsibilities as manager would affect his batting. Filing a surprisingly sarcastic game report from St. Louis at the end of July, Harrison humorously lamented the "piteous state of Mr. Rogers Hornsby during his temporary incumbency as manager of the Giants," which involved such "onerous duties" that against his former team he "had another feeble day at the bat and was barely able to summon a double and two singles." After the Rajah scored five runs in the Giants 13–2 victory over the third-place Cardinals, Harrison concluded, "It is now quite clear that John T. McGraw should hasten back at once and rescue Rogers from complete ruin."[19]

The result of the improved second-half play under Hornsby was that by the beginning of September the Giants, who had laid a seemingly permanent claim to fourth place, were emerging as favorites in a four-team pennant race. The team won ten straight games at the Polo Grounds, including a three-game sweep of the frontrunning Cubs, that left them in second place on Labor Day, only a game behind the Pirates, who had won seven consecutive games themselves. John Kiernan's "Sports of the *Times*" column on September 2 declared—after affirming McGraw's position as a baseball "mastermind"—that in the four team race, the Pirates and the Giants were the favorites because of their "heavy artillery." Then, crediting the Cardinals pitching and Joe McCarthy's own managerial savvy in Chicago, Kiernan decided that "only the seventh son of a seventh son could predict the outcome of this race."[20]

A pair of brothers would have the biggest impact on the race. Pittsburgh outfielders Paul and Lloyd Waner were abusing National League pitchers. Paul's 131 runs batted in led the league, while Lloyd's 133 runs scored were equal to Hornsby's at the top. Along with third baseman Pie Traynor, Pittsburgh claimed three players in the top five of the National League's batting averages. Paul would finish with a league-best average of .380, nineteen points better than Hornsby in second. And the Waners were at their best in September, as the Pirates posted eleven consecutive wins between the ninth and the seventeenth to put four and one-half games between themselves and the Giants and Cardinals, while the Cubs slowly faded from the race.

Even with the red-hot Pirates pulling ahead, the games between the contenders were fiercely contested. On succeeding days in games against the Cubs and Cardinals, the Giants saw two near riots. At Wrigley on September 12, the Cubs bettered the Giants 7–5 despite Hornsby's single, double, and home run in his three at-bats, though a close play at first base almost forced the game to an early end. In the bottom half of the eighth inning, Cubs fans in the bleachers showered rightfielder George Harper with bottles. With Harper taking cover in the bullpen, twelve members of the grounds crew spent five minutes clearing the bottles from the field. Then, with a runner on first, Cubs first baseman Charlie Grimm hit a groundball to Hornsby. Hornsby to Jackson to Terry went the double play, but when umpire Cy Pfirman called Grimm out, fans immediately aimed their bottles at him. It took the pleading of the Cubs coaches to quiet the fans and allow the game, which the home team was leading anyway, to continue.[21]

It was the players who caused a disturbance the next day in a double-header at Sportsman's Park. The animosity latent in a pennant race first showed itself when Larry Benton beaned former Giant Frisch, knocking him unconscious momentarily in the bottom of the first, an occurrence which the St. Louis fans, by now completely enamored of the Fordham Flash, booed loudly. Surprisingly, Frisch stayed in the game, and the tension remained high in the thick air of a late summer heat wave; temperatures were in the nineties and the stadium was full for over five hours. In the fourth inning, Cardinals shortstop Heinie Schuble tagged part-time left fielder Les Mann hard in the stomach on a play at second. Mann objected and began a shoving match, which subsequently emptied the dugouts. Under a new chorus of boos, the umpires calmed the players enough to resume play. Tempers cooled a bit, though the temperatures didn't, and the home team worked its way to a 5–2 victory. The second game belonged to the Giants offense, which knocked Jesse Haines off the mound in the first inning and tallied 12 total runs to win easily. The two pennant-chasing squads played seven games against one another in four days during the heat wave, and as they battered each other—the Giants won four games—the Pirates cruised ahead against second-division teams.

Three wins in four head-to-head games at Forbes Field brought the Giants back to within one and a half games of the leading Pirates. Hornsby hit a two-run home run in each half of a double-header on September 22; his homer provided the only runs in the first game, a 5–2 loss, but in the second game the home run sparked a big first inning and the Giants won easily, 7–1. Paul Waner played well in the double-header, but leadoff hitter Lloyd was hitless in 10 at-bats that day. The younger Waner had three hits the next day, though, to push Pittsburgh to a 5–0 lead. A hitless Hornsby watched happily as his team erased that lead, scoring six late runs to win. The Giants managed their third win in a row against the division leaders on Saturday, September 24, when Bill Terry tripled in the top of the ninth to drive in Hornsby to break a 1–1 tie.

The Giants returned to New York for one game in Brooklyn. The city was raging at the prospect of a cross-town World Series. "New York's New Babe Ruth" was completing a revival of the National League team that had disappointed the city with a sub-.500 record in 1926, while the original Babe, whose Yankees had already clinched the American League pennant again, was awing his fans as he approached his remarkable total of 60 home runs. A standing-room-only crowd turned out to see the Giants and Dodgers at Ebbets Field in Brooklyn, featuring McGraw's return to the dugout and the chance for the visitors to move into a virtual tie for first place. The crowd was so large and rowdy that police had to corral thousands who had spilled out into right field behind wooden dividers. The process of moving the pack was so tedious that the game was delayed over an hour; a 0–0 deadlock was stopped after seven innings due to darkness and declared an official draw.

The tie, followed by a loss to the hapless Phillies the next day, meant that instead of assuming first place, New York fell to third. Though the Giants won the next two games in Philadelphia, they failed to gain ground. Returning to Brooklyn, McGraw's pitchers surrendered 10 runs on September 30 to fall to 90–62, putting New York three games behind Pittsburgh with just two games left on the schedule. The Cardinals were eliminated from contention the following day after the Pirates defeated the Reds to capture their second pennant in three years. When the season's final games ended on October 2, the standings had Pittsburgh at 94–60, St. Louis at 92–61, and New York at 92–62. McCarthy's Cubs had fallen from the race and finished with 85 wins.

It was the Pirates second pennant in three years, and Hornsby, who was hired by the *Herald-Tribune* to report on the World Series, stated that he believed Pittsburgh's pitchers could slow the Yankees steamrolling offense enough to capture the title. Acknowledging Babe Ruth's dominant presence, Hornsby reminded several inquirers that he and his teammates had overcome a similar Yankee line-up the year before. Though without Hornsby the Cardinals failed to repeat their league championship, they had improved their win total from the 89–65 record they had achieved under the Rajah. Breadon was disappointed in the final standings—he would replace Bob O'Farrell at manager before the 1928 season—but was ecstatic that his team had actually improved after his controversial trade. St. Louis fans turned out to Cardinals games in record numbers again, and the team again turned a profit. Hornsby's stocks, it seems, were a good investment for the owner, who benefited at least as much from the National League's contributions to the settlement as Hornsby did. And the Giants, despite a few minor but testy conflicts between Hornsby the interim manager and the front office, seemed positioned to continue their success under McGraw and his heir apparent in the years to come.

Though he might not have realized it at the time, Hornsby's defense against the suit brought by Frank Moore would interfere with his future in New York. Despite the Rajah's predictions, the Yankees won their second ever championship in 1927, and after the Series Hornsby returned to St. Louis to be with his family and prepare for an October 31 trial date. Both sides arrived in court on Halloween and declared themselves ready to proceed, but a busy court docket forced the judge to postpone the trial until December 19. The family quickly departed for Texas to visit relatives, but with the affair at the front of his mind, Hornsby spoke with reporters at nearly every stop between St. Louis and Austin. Unable to comment specifically on the trial, Hornsby expressed confidence that

Moore could not prove his case, and instead answered baseball questions with his typical bluntness. He was repeatedly asked about his relationship with his friend and gambling buddy McGraw, and whether he planned to succeed Little Napoleon as manager. At this question, Hornsby's lifelong skepticism of baseball's front offices showed itself in his answers. Though he and Charles Stoneham had little interaction and even less business between them, on this trip Hornsby began to assert that he would not tolerate Stoneham and his assistants meddling in the manager's affairs and would not accept the manager's job unless there was a change in ownership.[22]

These comments undoubtedly reached Stoneham's office in New York quickly. The public comments from his employee combined with the owner's private dismay over Hornsby's trial led the owner to reconsider the celebrity-player's role with the Giants. The trial resumed on December 19 and lasted three days. Moore had reduced his initial suit for $70,075 to $45,075 and then again to $36,230, but Hornsby persisted with his claim that he owed the Kentucky bookie no money whatsoever. Moore asserted that between December 1925 and March 1926, when he was the Hornsbys' guest in San Antonio, he placed and financed bets for Hornsby totaling $327,995. Without openly denying that Moore told the truth or that the former Cardinal had failed to make good on over $70,000 worth of those bets, Hornsby's lawyer argued that he was not liable for the debts. Their circuitous reasoning was based on the grounds that gambling was illegal in Missouri and thus Moore's claim could not be sanctioned by the state courts. On December 21, after deliberating a mere hour and forty minutes, the jury returned a surprising verdict in Hornsby's favor.

In a curious means of appeal, Moore took his case to Judge Landis, asking that the commissioner use his power to force Hornsby to settle the debt. Landis, as vociferously as he chastised Hornsby for his gambling, refused to cooperate with the bookmaker. Landis abhorred gamblers and was working continuously to keep their influence out of Organized Baseball. Though he would not assist Moore, he undoubtedly spoke with Stoneham about Hornsby's continued interaction with the gambling world. On the other hand, Charles Stoneham did not abhor gambling. In fact, he often wagered in various venues himself, owned racehorses, and employed an avowed horseracing gambler as his team's manager for a quarter-century. Stoneham despised welchers. In Hornsby's trial, the Rajah proved he was a serious welcher, despite the jury's decision.

Stoneham's growing dislike of Hornsby coupled with his desire to consolidate his control of the Giants future. Just over a year after he had acquired the National League's best player—and Hornsby's frank distrust of ownership along with him—Stoneham rid himself of the Rajah. On January 10, 1928, Rogers Hornsby learned that he had been traded once again.

NOTES

1. "Everything Not So Pleasant in Cardinal Official Family," *Sporting News*, October 28, 1926, 1.

2. "'Hornsby Left No Alternative' Says Breadon Discussing Trade," *Sporting News*, December 23, 1926, 1.

3. Ibid.

4. Hornsby and Surface, *My War with Baseball*, 46.

5. Golenbock, *The Spirit of St. Louis: A History of the St. Louis Cardinals and Browns*, 121.

6. *St. Louis Post-Dispatch*, January 9, 1927, pt. 2, 1.

7. The information regarding Hornsby's stock settlement in this paragraph comes from typescript copies of John Heydler's correspondence on the matter. Rogers Hornsby Collection, National Baseball Library, Cooperstown, NY.

8. Arthur Daley, "He Who Gets Slapped," *New York Times*, September 18, 1953, 31.

9. Richard Vidmer, "Hornsby is Idol of His Own Ideal," *New York Times*, March 7, 1927, 23.

10. Ibid.

11. Richard Vidmer, "One-Man Job Keeps Two Cards Busy," *New York Times*, March 4, 1927, 17.

12. "Hornsby's .407 Batting Mark Tops Frisch's by 28 Points," *New York Times*, March 31, 1927, 19.

13. *Baltimore Sun*, April 3, 1927, clipping, Rogers Hornsby Collection, National Baseball Library, Cooperstown, NY.

14. Heydler correspondence, Rogers Hornsby Collection, National Baseball Library, Cooperstown, NY.

15. Frank Graham, "Hornsby Talks About His Case," April 4, 1927, clipping, Rogers Hornsby Collection, The Sporting News Archives, St. Louis, MO.

16. Heydler correspondence, Rogers Hornsby Collection, National Baseball Library, Cooperstown, NY.

17. Alexander, *Rogers Hornsby*, 134.

18. "McGraw to Quit, Hornsby to Get Job, West Hears," *New York Herald-Tribune*, June 16, 1927, clipping, Rogers Hornsby Collection, The Sporting News Archives, St. Louis, MO.

19. James R. Harrison, "Giants Beat Cards with Hornsby's Bat," *New York Times*, July 31, 1927, S1.

20. John Kieran, "Sports of the Times," *New York Times*, September 2, 1927, 13.

21. James R. Harrison, "Giants Down Cubs as Pop Bottles Fly," *New York Times*, September 13, 1927, 25.

22. James R. Harrison, "Hornsby Traded by Stoneham Alone," *New York Times*, January 13, 1928, 25.

Rogers Hornsby, with Jeannette and Billy Hornsby, at their farm in Robertson, Missouri, 1930. *National Baseball Hall of Fame Library, Cooperstown, N.Y.*

PEAKS AND VALLEYS

It is safe to say that Charles Stoneham did not trade Hornsby—he dumped him. The owner demanded little bounty for his best player as he briskly offered him around the league and dropped his asking price at each stop. From Brooklyn he sought Dazzy Vance and from Chicago outfielder Kiki Cuyler, but both teams were hesitant to assume Hornsby's massive contract. Cincinnati manager Jack Hendricks, a confirmed Hornsby-detractor since his days as manager of the Cardinals, blocked a trade that involved the minor cost of second baseman Hughie Critz and catcher Bubbles Hargrave. When Stoneham confirmed the trading of Hornsby to the Boston Braves, New York was shocked at the return their team had received for the Babe Ruth of the National League. Jimmie Welsh, a veteran player whose only comparison to the "Great Bambino" was that both played outfield and hit left-handed, and a rookie catcher named Shanty Hogan were the meager cost that Boston president Emil Fuchs paid to acquire the player journalists described as a superstar "beyond price."

Analyzing the second "amazing Hornsby deal" in just over a year, *Baseball Magazine* writer Franklin Lane refused to accept the trade as a mere personnel transaction. "Was this an even baseball trade?" Lane asked. "On the one side was Rogers Hornsby, a player once valued at a quarter of a million dollars by the Giants. Would they pay a quarter of a million dollars for Catcher Hogan and Outfielder Welsh? The idea is unthinkable." He goes on to assess what New York did receive. "Hogan is a player of promise. Smart baseball men have called him a comer. He may live to be the greatest catcher in the National League. But even so, his acquisition along with Outfielder Welsh hardly justifies the transfer of the greatest hitter, the greatest individual player in the league."[1]

There is little to add about the Giants return in the trade. Welsh would play only a season and a half for the Giants. Hogan provided John McGraw with a reliable catcher and a consistent headache: though he routinely hit over .300, Shanty was best known for his prodigious eating. McGraw flatly declared that his new backstop looked "like the back end of a truck," and surely enjoyed analyzing a racing form with Hornsby better than examining Hogan's restaurant receipts, which he would do for years.[2]

McGraw was leaving for his annual trip to Cuba when Stoneham and Fuchs made their deal, and it is unlikely that the New York owner did more than casually consult him. McGraw had been the primary decision-maker in personnel matters for years, but Stoneham was gradually taking responsibility for his team's roster and payroll. Stoneham was a novice to Organized Baseball when he bought the majority share in the New York club, but as his confidence in the sport increased, so did his intervention in the team's affairs. There were whispers around the league that McGraw, who had fallen into debt over ill-advised real estate investment in Florida, owed money to the team president. In any event, Stoneham had the final word in the organization. By 1928, he was willing to circumvent his legendary manager as he saw fit; as Lane put it, "when his mind is really made up on a certain course of action, he is willing to assume entire control."[3]

The manager said little about the trade publicly, and it seemed that his interests had been ignored. Stoneham based his explanation of the trade as a show of support for his McGraw, stating that he dealt Hornsby "in order to avoid any future conflict in the management of the club."[4] Before he could depart for Havana, reporters spoke with McGraw, who would not elaborate on his role in the deal, sticking to the phrase, "The trade has been made and there's all there is to it."[5] Hornsby, when questioned, refused to accept that McGraw contributed to the transaction. He testified to his professional respect and personal affection for his kindred baseball spirit, and wished McGraw would disavow taking part in the trade in person. "I would always be glad to take orders from him," Hornsby added.[6] The two wouldn't meet again until the opening game of the '28 season.

Giants fans reacted to news of the trade just as the St. Louis faithful had a year earlier. For weeks, the country's largest city berated Charles Stoneham's judgment and, like Hornsby, would not believe that McGraw could have acquiesced to the deal. Rumors arose that Stoneham actually owned a part of the Braves and had dealt Hornsby to Boston to strengthen his "other" team. The claims of "syndicate baseball" were taken to the offices of the league president and the commissioner, but John Heydler headed off the charges. "It is not within my province to investigate trades," Heydler announced. Further, he gave no "credence to the assertion that the Boston club is controlled by the Giants. Commissioner Landis looked into that charge years ago and found it to be false."[7]

If McGraw was displeased to lose the man he likely saw as his successor and New York fans were outraged to give up the league's best player, the Giants that remained surely shed no tears over their loss. They had played well under Hornsby's command, but their second baseman and part-time manager had been aloof in the clubhouse and, to their eyes, condescending as a leader. Fellow infielders Travis Jackson and Fred Lindstrom eagerly voiced their distaste for Hornsby to Stoneham, and after the trade to the press. Though they played for years with Bill Terry, a man equally difficult to like if not as imposing with his views, the future Hall-of-Famers never grew accustomed to the star second baseman that joined their team as captain and "future" manager. With career minor-leaguer Andy Cohen replacing Hornsby at second base, the Giants went on to win ninety-three games in 1928, finishing two games behind pennant-winning St. Louis.

Emil Fuchs was known as "Judge," though his fame on the bench was not quite as eminent as Commissioner Landis'. He had served as a circuit court magistrate in New York City for some time, but he was a baseball novice before investing in Boston's National League franchise. His investment had paid few dividends, as the organization lost money year after year. But Fuchs was a generous man who took genuine pleasure in owning a ballclub and treated his players and other employees with respect, even as they annually finished at the bottom of the league.[8] Boston's 60–94 record in 1927 was a mirror-image of Pittsburgh's pennant-winning mark. After dealing with Stoneham, the press roundly praised Fuchs for the courage to take on Hornsby's massive contract and ego in the hope that his talents could reverse the Braves' fortunes.

Fuchs opened his arms to Rogers Hornsby, going out of his way to make his main attraction welcome in Boston, offering a three-year contract to replace the two remaining on the Giants pact, and heeding any advice the veteran baseball man provided. The first recommendation Hornsby provided was for Lester Bell, his teammate and acolyte in St. Louis, who had been supplanted as Cardinals third baseman late in 1927 by Specs Toporcer. Fuchs sent his incumbent third baseman and $25,000 to Breadon for the dissatisfied Bell. Les, who truly enjoyed playing with the ornery Rajah, would go on to the second-best season of his career, coming close to the numbers he posted hitting behind Hornsby on the 1926 Cardinals.

Before he even considered the possibility of having Hornsby on board, Fuchs had released Dave Bancroft, a survivor of four seasons as the Braves' manager, and selected local man Jack Slattery, a successful skipper at Boston College and

Harvard, to replace him. At this point, Hornsby's reputation as a winning manager was without question, and speculation that he would become a player-manager arose around each team of which he was part. However, when he joined the Braves, just as when he became a Giant, Hornsby told anyone who would listen that he had no desire to manage, only to be a player in the ranks. Slattery, he announced to the press, would have his full support.

The manager would, at least, have access to Hornsby's ear. The two men were spring training roommates in St. Petersburg. To outside observers and to Fuchs, they appeared to get along, but teammates reported Hornsby's ambivalence to Slattery's suggestions from the start of practice at Coffee Pot Park. By the time the season was underway, ambivalence quickly turned toward antipathy.

Charles Alexander pithily summed up the Braves' season in his biography of the Rajah. "Early on, Hornsby may actually have entertained some notion that his presence . . . might make the Braves at least respectable. But while Hornsby would play up to form, so, unfortunately, would most of the rest of the team."9 By mid-May, Hornsby was hitting over .400 but the team was a mere 8–15. His frustration with the Braves' performance showed itself in his griping over Slattery's fruitless strategizing. His feelings toward the manager were similar to those he held toward Branch Rickey in St. Louis, and he often pejoratively called Slattery "collegiate." At the same time, Judge Fuchs was feeling out Hornsby's position on taking over as manager, but the player was hardly interested in tarnishing his managerial reputation by leading a group of teammates whose talents he openly doubted.

Not accustomed to managing professional players—particularly national stars who scoffed at his techniques—and discouraged by his 11–20 record, Jack Slattery resigned from the Braves on May 23. Fuchs was eager to get the star player he paid so handsomely to run the team as well. Hornsby, after much persuasion from the owner, agreed to be the new manager. He received no increase in pay for taking the hopeless position and probably accepted only out of deference to the kindly Fuchs and his own desire not to answer to another manager himself.

Just a few days after Slattery's resignation, Fuchs and Hornsby brought another St. Louis legend to Boston, trying to spark the sluggish offense. Released by the Washington Senators on the same day of the Braves' managerial change, former Brown George Sisler, now 35 years old and a two-time .400 hitter, cleared waivers and became the Braves' new first baseman. In his twenty games with the Senators, the 1922 American League MVP had only 12 hits and 2 runs batted in. At a cost of only $7,500, Sisler brought the Braves another veteran player and a consistent bat. He hit .340 and batted in 68 runs for Hornsby and company that season—he even stole 11 bases—and would close out his career in Boston two seasons later, keeping his average above .300 the entire time.

Sisler's contributions did little to counteract the efforts of the abysmal pitching staff. Three starting pitchers lost 17 or more games for the Braves in 1928, and the staff earned run average was an embarrassing 4.83. Further, a redesign of Braves Field in the off-season added bleachers and brought the outfield fence drastically closer to the plate in the misguided hope of increasing home runs and, indirectly, attendance. Home runs at Braves Field did become more common, but primarily for the visiting teams; two-thirds of all home runs hit in the first half of the season in the stadium were against Braves pitchers. Fuchs, sensing the negative impact on his team's morale, had the bleachers removed. Over the course of the season, the Braves gave up 100 home runs and hit only 52, nearly half coming off Hornsby's bat.

The result of their ineptitude was a 50–103 record for the Braves, good for a seventh place finish, 44½ games behind the Cardinals. It was their worst season—among many pitiful campaigns—since 1911 when they won 44 games and lost 107. For Hornsby, it was an embarrassment he actively tried to escape. By the end of the season, rumors were already traveling from Chicago to New York to Boston and back that Hornsby would be a Cub in 1929. For his part, a personally productive season at the plate allowed Hornsby to negotiate on his own behalf to improve his lot in regards to both his team and his pocketbook. In September, Fuchs signed his player-manager to a new contract for 1929–1931; it was the third three-year, $120,000 agreement Hornsby had signed in two seasons. With a new, guaranteed contract in hand, Hornsby campaigned with Joe McCarthy and Cubs president William Veeck Sr. to arrange a trade with Fuchs.

Shortly after the Yankees swept the Cardinals in the World Series, Fuchs placed a phone call to Hornsby, already back in St. Louis, to announce that he had solicited from the Cubs an offer of five players and a huge cash payment in exchange for the star. The Rajah told his friend and boss that, given the team's financial situation, he would "be a Goddam fool" to refuse it.[10] "There were several reasons given in the papers why I was traded," Hornsby recounted, "but I suggested the trade to Fuchs so he could have the money to get himself out of debt."[11] Announcement of the trade was held until after Massachusetts voters approved a measure that permitted professional sports contests to be held on Sundays. When the polls closed, Fuchs confirmed the trade with Veeck. The trade was formalized on November 7: Hornsby to Chicago for $200,000, pitchers Percy Lee Jones, Harry Seibold, and Bruce Cunningham; second baseman Freddy Maguire; and catcher Lou Leggett. Only Jones and Maguire had played on the Chicago major league team in 1928, but the minor league players held promise and had been expected to be full-time Cubs the next season. Most important, however, was the money, which immediately erased a good deal of Boston's debt. It was the single largest sum ever paid from one team to another for a player, surpassing the $125,000 the Yankees had given the Red Sox for Babe Ruth in 1920.

Even accounting for Charles Stoneham's urgency to move Hornsby and William Veeck's reluctance to part with Cubs regulars, Emil Fuchs performed a minor baseball miracle with his two transactions involving the Rajah. He had parlayed two average ballplayers (Welsh and Hogan to the Giants) into a season's worth of the league's best player (plus nearly a full season of managing at no extra cost), four everyday players, and a large step toward financial solvency. Though none of the new Boston players became stars, all but Leggett became regulars for the Braves. Jones and Seibold would each pitch about 200 innings in 1929 and Cunningham close to 100 in relief, while Maguire stepped into Hornsby's position in the field. He would hit only .251 in 1929 and remind no one of the previous second baseman at the plate, but he was an adept fielder who played about as well as Hornsby at his position.[12]

The annual trades of Hornsby were by now less surprising but no less newsworthy. Chicago papers, though not as enthusiastic in their welcome as New York had been two years before, were optimistic that Hornsby might provide a final offensive boost and a winner's experience to the talented Cubs, who had faded in the pennant chase for several years in a row. John Kieran of the *New York Times* said the team's new second baseman "won't be any more help to the Cubs than four wheels are to an automobile."[13] It seemed that the Rajah might also be a complement to hard-hitting and hard-drinking Hack Wilson, who was emerging as both a star and clubhouse headache. Of course, Hornsby's reputation as an aloof and belligerent teammate tempered most writers' expectations. Further, supporters of the Cubs popular manager Joe McCarthy were suspicious of Hornsby's record of replacing—some described it as undermining—his managers.

For the third consecutive year, Hornsby faced reporters covering his new team and revived his standard response to questions about his managerial aspirations. He was simply happy to be able to play for the Cubs, wanted to be a member of the team, respected Joe McCarthy, and was looking forward to a season without the added duties of managing. Given his forthrightness on all other matters, the press had little reason to doubt him even if history might have indicated otherwise. McCarthy was healthy, established, and consistently successful, and he had the strong support of both Cubs owner William Wrigley and Veeck. Hornsby insisted that he and McCarthy were already on "good terms" and that the pair "would get along without difficulty."

The Rajah was able to stay true to his word in 1929 because McCarthy gave him a wide berth and because the Cubs played very well. Though he had achieved typically bountiful statistics in Boston, his new surroundings and teammates provided a situation similar to the offensive resurgence he had experienced with the Giants. The 1928 Braves were easily the worst set of players that Hornsby shared the field with during his playing career. Despite the kindness and deference Emil Fuchs showed his player-manager during their brief time together, Hornsby certainly saw a mutual benefit to the trade he engineered with the Cubs. Fuchs and the Braves received their much needed financial relief while Hornsby found his way back to a team with pennant hopes and championship-caliber players. Recounting his first season in Chicago, Hornsby would declare that "the Cubs had the best group of individual players of any team I ever played on."[14]

An extremely talented roster justified hopes for the first Chicago pennant in a decade. From the top to the bottom of the line-up, the Cubs were a balanced team with speed, power, and consistency. Hornsby's new double-play companion and roommate Woody English was a steady leadoff hitter, and first baseman Charlie Grimm was respected for his vacuum of a glove and his even temper. The outfield, led by three-time home run champion Wilson, was the best in baseball and provided a powerful heart to the line-up; McCarthy decided that Hornsby would bat fourth, behind rightfielder Kiki Cuyler, with Wilson and leftfielder Riggs Stephenson to follow. The pitching rotation was also promising: Pat Malone had won eighteen games as a rookie in 1928, and veterans Charlie Root and Guy Bush were regular winners as well.

William Wrigley was ready to see his investment in the Cubs pay off. Wrigley had just spent several hundred thousand dollars to expand his eponymous field to 40,000 seats and paid more for a player than any owner in history had before. "I have spent several million dollars trying to get a team like this," he said before the 1929 season. "But I believe it will realize a dream for me—a National League pennant for Chicago. If we don't win the pennant—well, we'll try harder next year. But I have a hunch the team will deliver this time."[15]

Mob wars raged through the streets of Chicago as Hornsby and teammates set off for Catalina Island, California—his fifth spring training destination in as many years. Detailed accounts of the murderous rampages of Al Capone's henchmen and the retributive killings by the Irish crime syndicate buried predictions for the Cubs season deep in the Chicago papers. While writers nationwide predicted the fifth New York–versus–New York World Series of the decade, the positive reports on the new Cub waned out of the sports pages, replaced by myriad predictions for Hornsby-fueled dissension. The obvious lifestyle differences between Hornsby and Wilson's gang, as well as the second managerial mind in the clubhouse, were sure to create quite a drama, regardless of what the actors themselves might say. Yet the Cubs trained well together, even merrily. As it had for the last few years, the bustle of the off-season had Hornsby anxious just to play baseball again. He also went out of his way to be a model teammate. He was especially proud when a Chicago paper reported on his training habits, noting that he was usually the first player to the practice field, listened attentively to McCarthy, and was friendly toward the whole team, even calling "all the rookies by their nicknames, high-hatting none."[16]

The good feelings lasted all season: winning, as it often did in the Rajah's career, proved to be an excellent gel for a team of mismatched personalities. McCarthy's squad battled for the season's first four months in a three-team clinch at the top of the standings. Perennial pennant contenders Pittsburgh and New York routinely traded places with the Cubs as Hornsby warmed up to his new surroundings. Contests between any pair of the contenders drew huge crowds even early in the season. On a stormy day in May, 55,000 fans squeezed into the Polo Grounds to watch the Cubs and Giants for eleven innings before weather stopped the game at a 6–6 tie. Chicago's second baseman trailed a few of his teammates in batting average for the first part of the season, but by June Hornsby assumed the role of offensive leader he had been acquired to fill.

Anecdotes about Hornsby's unshakeable poise at the plate cropped up throughout his career. With his stroke back in top form, a new one spread through the ranks of sportswriters nationwide. Back in Boston where his former teammates were keenly aware of his power, Braves catcher Al Spohrer attempted to distract the Great Rajah at the plate. Having witnessed Hornsby's passion for thick milkshakes and thicker steaks, he started a conversation from his squat.

"Say, Rog," Spohrer said, "my wife has discovered a butcher who sells great steaks."

"That so?" Hornsby inquired as the umpire called the first pitch a strike.

"Not only that, but my wife can cook a steak better than anyone I know. Grace really knows how to broil 'em."

Another strike was called as Hornsby politely responded, "Mmm. Sounds good."

"What Grace and I thought," continued Spohrer as the third pitch was delivered, pleased he had Hornsby's attention, "was that the next time you're in Boston, Rog, you might come to the house and have a steak with us."

Hornsby drove the ball into the left field bleachers and trotted around the bases. At home plate he turned to the catcher.

"What night shall we make it, Al?"[17]

In all of June and July his average jumped by 20 points and he hit 16 home runs in addition to the one in Boston. Along with Wilson's 28-game hitting streak, Hornsby's offensive explosion led his team to 18 wins in 20 games, propelling them from 2 games behind Pittsburgh to 7½ games ahead. The Cubs would never look back as they ran away with the pennant.

Once again, Hornsby's season was the best in the National League, but this year it was part of a magnificent team performance. The Rajah played in every game, scored a National League record 156 runs and batted in 149. And though Chuck Klein of the Phillies broke Hornsby's league record of 42 home runs by one, the Chicago second baseman had 39 of his own. The bonus of Hornsby's fine season, which earned him his second Most Valuable Player award, was that the team around him hit nearly as well as he did. All three Cubs outfielders hit better than .340 with more than 100 RBIs; Wilson matched Hornsby's 39 home runs and even knocked in 10 more runs than his teammate.

Hornsby had proven to be the spark Chicago needed; suspicion that he was an "underminer" was replaced with praise of his constant leadership. McCarthy acknowledged that Hornsby's experience and passion for the game had helped stabilize his excitable team. In a profile of McCarthy, writer John Drebinger noted the veteran's influence on the team. "One scarcely has to know the Rajah five minutes to appreciate that he lives, breathes and dreams baseball. That same spirit seems to pervade the entire Cubs team," Drebinger reported.[18]

The country had plenty of time to prepare for the World Series in 1929, because the Philadelphia Athletics and the Cubs had both won their respective pennants by wide margins. Weeks of anticipation had Cubs supporters in the Midwest and A's fans on the East Coast champing at the bit for the Series to begin. Philadelphia's record in the American League was 104–46 and they finished some eighteen games ahead of the second-place Yankees. Despite the impressive regular season record of Connie Mack's team, the Series ahead seemed evenly matched.

Previews of the Fall Classic pointed out that Hornsby and the Cubs trio of outfielders were perfectly poised to counter the potent bats of Jimmie Foxx, Al Simmons, and Mickey Cochrane. Further, though Lefty Grove and George Earnshaw had each won more than twenty games for Philadelphia, Chicago's Charlie Root and Pat Malone were pitching as well as anyone in the game that autumn. The Yankees had swept the previous two championship series, but it seemed that this October would provide an even contest. It was hardly so.

In over-filled Wrigley Field, temporarily expanded to some 50,000 seats, the A's won a close first game behind unknown right-hander Howard Ehmke, who had managed only one victory all season in just eleven appearances. Ehmke did not surrender a run until the bottom of the ninth and his unorthodox delivery baffled the home team. He struck out a record thirteen batters—Hornsby twice.

Jimmie Foxx's 2-run homer in the top of the ninth, off an effective but unfortunate Guy Bush, made the difference in the 3–1 victory. The two Athletics aces, Earnshaw and Grove, combined their strengths in Game 2, as they each struck out Hornsby once and together held Chicago to 3 runs. Home runs by Foxx and left fielder Simmons propelled Philadelphia to an easy 9–3 win.

In Philadelphia two nights later, the Cubs finally came alive. Because of his strong first performance, McCarthy decided to pitch Bush again in Game 3. Hornsby struck out two more times, but his sixth-inning single tied the game and he scored one of his team's 3 runs. Those tallies were plenty for Bush, who kept Simmons and Foxx hitless, and the Cubs earned the National League's first World Series victory since Hornsby tagged out Ruth to end Game 7 in 1926.

The Athletics would not be stopped however. The most embarrassing moment for Chicago came in Game 4 at Philadelphia, an event that would be described as "the greatest debacle, the most terrific flop, in the history of the world series."[19] Charlie Root had kept the A's in check with only 3 hits in six innings, while his team had breezed to 8 easy runs off of three Philadelphia pitchers. In the bottom of the seventh, though, things collapsed. Simmons hit the inning's first pitch into the left-field stands, ending the shutout. Root then allowed 4 consecutive singles. With 1 out and 4 runs in, McCarthy changed pitchers. An inside-the-park home run by Mule Haas on a botched play by Hack Wilson added three runs, and after another pitching change, Foxx's second single of the inning drove in Cochrane with the tying score. McCarthy finally resorted to Pat Malone, scheduled to pitch the next game, who promptly loaded the bases and then gave up a 2-run double. The inning mercifully ended with the Athletics ahead 10–8. The next six Cubs batters were retired in order—Hornsby made the final out—and Chicago's spirit was destroyed. A 3–2 Philadelphia win in Game 5 on October 14 sealed the fourth world championship of Connie Mack's career.

In the second and final World Series of Rogers Hornsby's career, he had again played very poorly. His uncharacteristic performance yielded only 5 hits in 21 at-bats and he struck out 8 times—one of the worst five-game stretches in his career to that point. Though the Cubs piled up fifty strikeouts as a team and were uniformly bad, Hornsby blamed himself for making such a large contribution to the team's flat play.

He did not acknowledge as much to teammates or reporters, but over the final month of the season, he had endured sharp pains in his right foot. Back in St. Louis after the Series, he learned that he could attribute his limited mobility in the field—and weakness pushing off his back leg in the batter's box—to bone spurs on his heel. Dr. Robert Hyland took the National League's Most Valuable Player into surgery in late November. He removed the calcification from Hornsby's heel, alleviating the pain temporarily. Unfortunately, Hyland had no means to prevent recurrence of a condition that would plague the Rajah for the rest of his playing career.

Hornsby also suffered a financial injury in the aftermath of the 1929 season; as it did for most of the country's investors, the October stock market crash took a huge chunk out of the wealth Hornsby had accumulated. He was already suffering through various gambling losses, a few ill-advised investments, and the uneven success of his farming ventures when the crash occurred, and Hornsby lost on what he later described as the biggest gamble of his life. His investment in the Radio Corporation of America (RCA), which had funded his purchase of the Missouri farm and a number of large racing wagers during the market's boom, disappeared instantly. "I lost a lot more money in Wall Street than I ever did on the race track," he said. "The truth is, I lost . . . $100,000 worth in one lump at one time."[20]

His physical and financial ailments spoiled his off-season at his Robertson home and made news of his second BBWAA Most Valuable Player award anti-climactic. His only contact with the ballclub he had inspired to a pennant was a short trip to Veeck's office, in which he showed the club president the results of his surgery and persuaded him to sign the steadfast Lester Bell to play third base.

Hornsby arrived in California for spring training in 1930 uncertain of his condition but anxious to shed his winter doldrums. He left a week later on crutches unsure when he would get to play at all. Chicago doctors examined his heel and said they had no way to treat it, but that he would likely do no more damage by playing. He sat out the rest of spring training, but dutifully took the field with the pennant favorites when the season started April 15. The season would be remembered as the year of the second recognizable "juicing" of the regulation Spalding since the dead ball era; the cumulative batting average of the whole National League was .303, but the best hitter of the 1920s would not share the benefits. While the rest of the league started to hit the "jackrabbit" balls all over the country's stadiums, Hornsby struggled.

The mighty Rajah would only appear in forty-seven games for the 1930 Cubs, getting just 104 at-bats and managing just 2 home runs to go with his .308 average. In and out of the lineup over the season's first two months, Hornsby had yet to pull his average over .300 when he experienced another frustrating injury. One day before Cubs officials had arranged to present him with the MVP award, he made an awkward slide into third base and broke his left ankle. On May 31, with one foot in a cast and the other still tender from his bone spurs, Hornsby hobbled to home plate to accept his $1,000 and his medallion. His teammates, playing well despite the sudden death of relief pitcher Hal Carlson and the injuries to Hornsby, beat the Cardinals for their fourth straight win while Hornsby boarded a train bound for St. Louis.

He convalesced in a wheelchair at his Missouri farm for two months, enjoying the company of Jeannette and Billy and keeping his mind off of baseball. He surely felt frustration when news reached him that the Cubs had risen from third in the standings to first on the strength of Hack Wilson's record pace of runs batted in. Even more infuriating were rumors that his teammates, bolstered by their recent winning streak, felt he was superfluous to their success. The polite distance McCarthy had kept during the year before also now seemed cold, and Hornsby heard that he might even be traded again.

William Wrigley had no intention to trade his $200,000 investment, however. In fact, some of McCarthy's coldness toward Hornsby could be attributed to the warm praise for the MVP's baseball savvy that Wrigley repeated in front of his manager. Without a contract for 1931, McCarthy suspected that he—and not Hornsby—would be gone the next season. Hornsby returned to Chicago at the beginning of September and tested his feet in a few games, but manager and player spoke very little. The Rajah had rarely questioned McCarthy's tactics in public or in private, but, thanks to Wrigley's affection for Hornsby, the two were inevitably alienated.

Under first-year manager Gabby Street, the red-hot St. Louis Cardinals breezed past the Dodgers, the Giants, and then the Cubs to clinch their third National League title in five years. Meanwhile, McCarthy's hold on his job evaporated; without a repeat pennant, he had failed in Wrigley's eyes. With the Cubs in Boston and four games against Cincinnati remaining in the season, Wrigley made front-page news when he announced that he and Veeck had "simply decided to make a change." Rogers Hornsby, he said, would manage the Cubs in 1931.[21] Subsequently, McCarthy refused to finish the season, so Hornsby, withdrawn from the line-up because of his ankle, took over for the final four games. The Cubs swept the season-ending series from the Reds in Wrigley Field before a Chicago faithful with mixed emotions about the new manager.

Watching Hornsby take control of his fourth major league team, reporters quickly noted the recurring theme of his managerial career, though he repeatedly assured anyone who would listen that he had never "undermined" his manager and that "McCarthy and I parted friends."[22] A few writers claimed private evidence that Hornsby questioned McCarthy's judgment, but others simply speculated that a change could not have occurred without the Rajah jockeying for another chance to manage. Erstwhile McCarthy supporter Gordon Mackay of the *Philadelphia Record* insisted that "Hornsby did nothing to make the road easy for McCarthy." He further claimed that in 1930 the injured second baseman had been malingering, "content to take his time until Wrigley made McCarthy walk the plank and put the Rajah in command."[23]

Another McCarthy defender had a financial insight into the change that did not seem unreasonable. In the *Sporting News*, Rud Rennie pointed out that Hornsby was under a guaranteed contract at $40,000 per year and had cost Wrigley quite a sum to acquire. If the Rajah's damaged heel was going to prevent him from returning the investment on the field, Wrigley needed to make use of his managerial talents and save himself McCarthy's $35,000 salary. Rennie concluded that "having killed the plain goose that layed [*sic*] the golden eggs, Mr. Wrigley will try a golden goose."[24]

The speculation was certainly justified, but it is possible that Wrigley simply could not resist making Hornsby his manager. The Rajah had impressed the chewing gum magnate since their first meetings as owner and player. Wrigley had grown tired of Hack Wilson and his friends making drunken spectacles of themselves around Chicago, and he did blame McCarthy for his lack of control. He admired the clean-living Hornsby and felt his reputation as a disciplined leader would be the difference in returning the Cubs to the World Series. Furthermore, he liked the way Hornsby talked about his sport. "I heard more baseball today than I have heard in my whole life," he said after one of his first conversations with the star hitter.[25]

Hornsby tried to bring a new attitude to the team in spring training at the recently constructed Wrigley Field in California. Aside from the newly wealthy Hack Wilson who had received the second biggest contract in the league—behind Hornsby—the Cubs were mostly suspicious of their teammate and manager. Charlie Grimm had heard Hornsby was trying to replace him with Jim Bottomley, and several others were simply angry to be without McCarthy. Their former manager had not stayed unemployed long, replacing Miller Huggins's successor Bob Shawkey in New York, and a postseason contest between Chicago and McCarthy's Yankees seemed possible.

Even after the abuse he absorbed from the press during the off-season, Hornsby regularly entertained reporters' questions from his evening perch in the hotel lobby. Los Angeles writer Paul Mickelson found the blunt Hornsby to be "one of the most difficult men in sport to interview"; after sitting with the manager, he came to understand that he would "answer questions fully and clearly but volunteers little information."[26] The trick was to probe him with a real baseball question, perhaps even regarding the quality of his own players. He would then speak at length—and quite frankly, to the lucky reporter's delight. Another reporter decided that the Rajah didn't "believe in calling a spade simply a spade when there are words much blacker."[27]

Near the end of spring training on Catalina Island, however, Hornsby was in good spirits. Tough as always on his players, he had returned to the training methods he employed as Cardinals manager in 1926. The long practices and dedication to winning each game had actually focused the team on their play rather than on McCarthy's plight, he believed, and the regimen seemed to have improved his ailing heel. As the team was getting ready to depart, he was ready to ignore his critics and have a bit of fun, and he found an easy target in a California radio man. He agreed to a live interview in Pasadena after one of the last preseason games, and the broadcast began a recap of his career and record and then moved to his assessment of the Cubs chances to win another pennant. The conversation then turned to the team's spring training success before the announcer said, "You've trained all over the country, Mr. Hornsby. Would you agree that California is just about the best place in the world to train a major-league ball club?" Hornsby abruptly shot back, "Nope. San Antonio," and chuckled at the stupified reporter.[28]

The Chicago Cubs left spring training focused but not entirely satisfied with their new manager. Hornsby, ready to get back to the field, decided he could not care less. When his friend, writer Sid Keener, asked him about the tangible dissension on the club, the Rajah was typically frank in his judgment of the men he was set to lead. "Between us," he told Keener on the record, "I'll be in the National League when many players on this club are in the minors."[29]

NOTES

1. Franklin C. Lane, "The Amazing Hornsby Deal," *Baseball Magazine*, March 1928, 435.

2. Bill James, *The New Bill James Historical Baseball Abstract* (New York: Free Press, 2001), 426.

3. Lane, "The Amazing Hornsby Deal," 436.

4. John Drebinger, "Hornsby Deal Made 'To Avoid Conflict,'" *New York Times*, January 12, 1928, 34.

5. Ibid.

6. Ibid.

7. Harrison, "Hornsby Traded By Stoneham Alone," 25.

8. From 1920 through 1927 the Braves finished last or next to last six times.

9. Alexander, *Rogers Hornsby*, 145.

10. Hornsby, *My Kind of Baseball*, 100.

11. Hornsby and Surface, *My War with Baseball*, 47.

12. Less successful than Fuchs' trading efforts was his decision to install himself as field manager in 1929. He was the first person with no professional playing experience

to manage in the National League and, even with legendary player Johnny Evers as his assistant, Fuchs' ineptitude was sadly obvious. He removed himself from the dugout in May 1929, though he remained manager nominally for the whole of the season.

13. John Kieran, "Sports of the Times," *New York Times*, March 31, 1929, 146.

14. Hornsby and Surface, *My War with Baseball*, 48.

15. "Spent Millions on Cubs, Wrigley Now Sees Pennant," *New York Times*, April 17, 1929, 31.

16. Hornsby and Surface, *My War with Baseball*, 47.

17. Bob Broeg, "Broeg on Baseball" column, *St. Louis Post-Dispatch*, August 12, 1972, clipping Rogers Hornsby, The Sporting News Archives, St. Louis. This anecdote appears in a variety of forms in dozens of columns on Hornsby.

18. John Drebinger, "Joe McCarthy—Specialist in Managing," *New York Times*, September 13, 1929, 34.

19. *Chicago Tribune*, October 10, 1929, 16.

20. F. C. Lane, "Rogers Hornsby Springs a New Sensation," *Baseball Magazine*, September 1933, 443; Sher, "Rogers Hornsby: The Mighty Rajah," 63.

21. *Chicago Tribune*, September 23, 1930, 1.

22. *Chicago Tribune*, January 11, 1931, 2.

23. *Philadelphia Record* [August 1931], clipping, Rogers Hornsby Collection, The Sporting News Archives, St. Louis.

24. *Sporting News*, October 2, 1930, 2.

25. Alexander, *Rogers Hornsby*, 153.

26. Associated Press report, February 24, 1931, clipping, Rogers Hornsby Collection, The Sporting News Archives, St. Louis.

27. [June 30, 1932], clipping, Rogers Hornsby Collection, National Baseball Library, Cooperstown, NY.

28. J. Roy Stockton, Foreword to Hornsby, *My Kind of Baseball*, 22. There are as many versions of this story as there are writers who repeat it.

29. Sid Keener, "Sid Keener's Column," *St. Louis Star* [1931], Rogers Hornsby Collection, The Sporting News Archives, St. Louis.

8

THE GREAT DEPRESSION

Rogers Hornsby's stint as manager of the Chicago Cubs was the longest of his three formal roles in the position to that point; it lasted only a season and a half, however. Although the team he managed was as ill-behaved as any club he had ever been a part of, Hornsby was growing less tolerant as he got older, too. Nearly 35 years old, he was hungry for a chance to win another championship but physically less able to contribute to his team's cause. The combination of his frustration with his ailments and his exasperation at his teammates' rowdy behavior made him a curt and surly leader. As a result, his Cubs were good but not great, staying near the top of the National League throughout his short tenure but unable or unwilling to win for the Rajah.

The 1931 season began well. Throughout the previous year, Hornsby had ballooned to 200 pounds due to the inactivity from his injuries. His spring training regimen reduced his weight 10 percent and made him feel 100 percent better. He put himself in the line-up at Wrigley Field on April 14, hitting fourth and playing second; it was his sixteenth consecutive Opening Day start. The Cubs won three games out of four against the Pittsburgh Pirates to begin the year, and their player-manager hit home runs in two of the victories. A week later at Forbes Field, Hornsby's 3 home runs in consecutive plate appearances accounted for eight of the team's ten scores in another victory over the Pirates. With practically a whole season lost to injuries, the mighty Rajah was back on top of the National League.

As per the instructions of the league presidents, the Spalding Company had re-modified their baseballs to counteract the previous season's scoring upsurge.

No player felt the change more dramatically than Hack Wilson. He had truly earned the raise to $35,000 per year he received after his 56 home run, 191 RBIs performance in 1930, but he endured a season-long slump under Hornsby in 1931 that effectively ended his career. Wilson attributed his troubles at the plate to the deadened baseball; Hornsby attributed them to Hack's worsening alcoholism.

Chicago sportswriter Warren Brown said that Wilson "was a high-ball hitter on the field, and off it."[1] Although Hornsby never drank himself, after positive experiences with his good friend Grover Alexander, he had said he did not care what a man did or did not imbibe, so long as it never interfered with his play. In 1931, due to his long nights in Chicago's speakeasies, Wilson hit his favored high pitches for easy fly outs instead of home runs. And so, for the first time as a manager, Hornsby enforced an in-season curfew.

Wilson may have needed the discipline, but he and the other Cubs resented Hornsby's shortening of the long leash McCarthy had issued, especially because Hornsby seemed to take pleasure in policing the team's habits. Once, when Wilson, pitcher Pat Malone, and part-time catcher Rollie Hemsley snuck out after curfew for a night of carousing in Manhattan, Hornsby made an example of "Rollicking Rollie." Returning to the hotel near dawn, Hemsley knew better than to take the elevator because Hornsby's room was nearby. So, after climbing fifteen flights of stairs, he opened a door to find his manager smiling at him. "Did you have fun, Rollie?" he was asked, to which Hemsley sheepishly nodded in the affirmative. "That's good. I was hoping you'd have fun," Hornsby continued. "I was hoping you'd have 350 dollars worth of fun, because that's exactly the amount I'm fining you."[2]

The team dipped in the standings, and every infraction by the players and every reprimand by Hornsby chilled the clubhouse further. Even his friend Woody English felt apprehensive around the manager. To make matters worse, Hornsby's heel was hurting again: His range at second base was severely limited, he could not turn double plays effectively, and he lacked power in his swings at outside pitches. Though he hit 2 home runs in an easy win at Philadelphia on June 30, his average dropped from close to .360 to under .330. He put himself on the bench for an Independence Day double-header at Wrigley Field and went in and out of the line-up for the rest of the season—and the rest of his playing career, it would turn out.

With their grouchy player-manager on the bench most of July, the Cubs deteriorated. Hornsby benched Wilson at the same time as himself and devoted a large amount of energy to enforcing his training rules. To make matters worse, after the team fell from three and one-half games behind St. Louis to nine and one-half back in the month, Riggs Stephenson broke his ankle against the

Phillies on July 28. Pennant hopes were lost and some quickly called for Hornsby's termination, but Wrigley and Veeck defended their manager.

The Rajah had to answer questions that his players struggled because of, rather than in spite of, his guidance. "All I've asked of the fellows is to play ball," he told Sid Keener. "I don't write their salaries. They write their own ticket. Mr. Wrigley is paying them good money." He believed that his players took the field "leveling with full speed. Why shouldn't they? It's their own bread and butter." Pressed by his reporter friend on the public perception that his players were tanking games to get him fired, he replied, "Do you think they're loafing on the job because they don't like my system? That's silly."[3]

Loafing or not, the Cubs limped to the end of the season. Hornsby rarely played, and Hack Wilson reached a breaking point. After another raucous night in New York, Wilson missed curfew and was caught by his manager. Hornsby, exasperated, told his outfielder to take the next train back to Chicago. The penitent Hack apologized in front of the whole team, however, and Hornsby allowed him to stay on for the road trip, but he would not start Wilson in a game again. Rookie outfielder Vince Barton had to leave the team briefly to attend his father's funeral, leaving the team with only three regular outfielders for a series in Cincinnati. But rather than start Wilson, Hornsby had him sit in the bullpen to warm up relievers and placed pitcher Bud Teachout in left field. The National League's home run and RBIs record holder was sorely embarrassed.

On the train from Cincinnati back to Chicago September 5, Wilson and his drinking buddy Malone accosted two sportswriters who were traveling with the team. The four men argued about the players' representation in the papers for a while before Malone, with Wilson hooting encouragement, punched both men. The writers and Hornsby reported the incident to William Veeck, who fined Malone $500 and suspended Wilson for the remainder of the schedule. William Wrigley spoke to reporters and "said he wanted Wilson sold or traded, adding that it was a 'personal wish.'"[4] With a .261 average and just 13 home runs, Wilson's season was over and his future as a Cub in serious doubt.

After Wilson's suspension, the team won more games than it lost, thanks to an eight-game winning streak at Wrigley Field. In a game against the Braves during that streak, Hornsby pinch-hit himself in the eleventh inning and connected on a home run with the bases loaded; historian David Vincent believes Hornsby's shot was the first extra-inning grand slam in major league history.[5] It was a high point in an otherwise disastrous end to the year for the once-mighty Rajah, who resigned himself to the fact that he would likely never play regularly again. His future was in managing, he thought, though his record in his second complete season as a manager was 84–70, respectable enough but a disappointing seventeen games worse than Gabby Street's Cardinals, the eventual World Series winners.

Wrigley, Veeck, and Hornsby unanimously decided to trade Wilson to St. Louis in early December when Branch Rickey indicated that the champions would be willing to part with veteran pitcher Burleigh Grimes. Chicago needed to be rid of Wilson, and Hornsby wanted pitching depth. Meanwhile, the difficult financial state of the country influenced Sam Breadon to cut costs, and Rickey decided that Grimes was the most expendable of his high-priced players, despite his two wins over the Athletics in the World Series—a team many believed to be the best of Connie Mack's long tenure. On December 9, 1931, the deal was announced, Grimes to Chicago for Wilson and Bud Teachout.

Wilson was ecstatic, and the subsequent attention the trade received from the press gave him the opportunity to sound off on his unsuccessful year. He had slumped because of Hornsby's requirement that batters take two balls–no strikes and three balls–one strike pitches, he said. There had no been no way to succeed under the stubborn Rajah, because players were "not allowed to hit." Freed of Hornsby's control, he predicted his own motivated resurgence and sneered at his detractors. "You can say for me that I will be out there next season to show Hornsby and the others that they had been wrong."[6] Breadon joined in the attack, telling New York reporters that he expected Hack to play well "just to show up Hornsby and the Cubs."[7]

The Cardinals owner was committed to reducing his team's budget, though. Armed with the evidence of Wilson's pathetic season and late-night carousing, Breadon made a firm offer to his new outfielder of only $7,500 for the season, less than a quarter of his previous salary. Hack scoffed at the deal. Breadon, comfortable with the defending champion's roster, promptly sold him to Brooklyn for $45,000 and a minor league pitcher. In the New York borough, Wilson received a respectable $16,000 salary and made a notable comeback, hitting near .300 with 23 home runs and 123 runs batted in, fourth best in the league. Hornsby's assessment of him would ultimately prove correct, however, as the self-destructive Hack drank himself out of the league within two years.

The winter of 1931–1932 was a mournful one for Chicago sports, as the city lost the owners of both its major league franchises. Late in October, the president of the White Sox and popular South Side figure Charley Comiskey died. Within three months, the North Side chewing gum magnate William Wrigley passed away as well, at his home in Phoenix, Arizona. Thousands of Chicago's residents thronged each man's memorial; Hornsby traveled from his farm to attend the service in honor of his owner and advocate. In fact, Wrigley's death meant that Hornsby had lost his closest ally in Chicago, and at the memorial he remembered the Cubs owner as "the best boss I ever had."[8] Both Comiskey and Wrigley left their franchises to their sons, and so Hornsby's new boss would be Philip Wrigley, who quickly advertised that he knew and cared little about baseball. William Veeck, he said, was capable of operating the Cubs on his own.

Veeck and Hornsby had no quarrel with one another when spring training began in March. They were allies in an effort to return the Cubs to the pennant and Cubs fans to the Wrigley Field seats. The continued success of the franchise, Veeck told his manager, depended on the team maintaining their fans' support. In 1930, Chicago had set a major league record for attendance during their attempt to defend the pennant, but the next season, even though the Cubs again drew more paying customers than any other team, attendance dropped by more than 500,000 tickets. Such a trend could not continue, regardless of the country's financial situation. Hornsby agreed, and he told Veeck that his pitching staff could carry Chicago to the pennant and bring fans to the ballpark.

Hornsby was especially pleased to be reunited with Grimes, his teammate on the Giants in 1927. The Rajah considered Burleigh a kindred spirit. "He says what he thinks and says it where he thinks it and I like a man like that," he told St. Louis writer J. Roy Stockton. "And when he says something he says it with the one purpose of winning."[9] Grimes' winning attitude would be contagious to the other pitchers, the manager thought, and he expected each of his five starters to win at least fifteen games in '32. Four Cubs pitchers did win at least fifteen games, led by the inexperienced Lon Warneke's 22 wins, but Grimes was not one of them. He and Hornsby were alike both in their spirit and their waning health that year.

For the first time in his career, the Rajah did not play on Opening Day. He had been mostly inactive throughout the off-season and his heel bothered him constantly, so he was desperately out of shape and as heavy as he had ever been that April. He kept his attention on managing and planned to pinch-hit when he felt able. In his place at second base he started Billy Herman, whom Hornsby decided would be his permanent replacement. The Cubs started fast, despite Hornsby's absence, Riggs Stephenson's stubborn ankle fracture, and new injuries to Woody English and Kiki Cuyler. Culyer's injury—he broke a bone in his foot April 24—was expected to heal quickly, but when his recovery seemed to be dragging on and the outfield suffered without him, Hornsby decided to get himself back into the line-up.

Though he had not spent even an inning in the outfield since 1921, he put himself in right field on May 30 for a double-header against the Pirates. The teams split and he felt comfortable while getting a hit in each game, so the next day, when the Cardinals arrived for another double-header, he headed out to right field again. He was hitless in Grimes's morning loss, but his home run and double in the afternoon game accounted for the decisive runs in a 6–2 victory.

It would be his only home run that season, for after some embarrassing moments in the outfield during the next three games, he withdrew from the line-up and allowed himself only forty more at-bats.

Along with a few other substantial reasons, such as his increasingly terse manner with his players and his disregard of Veeck's recommendations, Hornsby's reluctance to put himself into games led to his midseason dismissal. In the ninth inning of a game against Hack Wilson and the Dodgers, Hornsby pinch-hit for his pitcher with Frank Demaree, a hot prospect bought from a Pacific Coast League team for a reported $50,000. Demaree popped up to end the game. Veeck, on the road with the team at the time, asked Hornsby why he had put Demaree into such a difficult spot instead of batting himself. The manager replied that Veeck had asked for Hornsby to "look over" the young player to "see if he was worth paying all that money for," and thus he figured Veeck "didn't mean for me to look him over in the dining room or playing fan tan."[10] The club president fumed privately and summoned Charlie Grimm to his hotel room, asking the team captain and first baseman if he would take over as manager should Hornsby be fired. Grimm said he surely would, and Hornsby's fate was sealed.

In Philadelphia on August 2, a week after Demaree's controversial debut, Veeck and Hornsby met with the press to announce that Hornsby had agreed to "step out as manager."[11] The team was 54–36, in second place by five games behind the league-leading Pirates, and Hornsby was "leaving the club," he said, due to "big differences of opinion about the ball club and the way it should be handled."[12] Veeck would only elaborate to say that Hornsby had cleared waivers as a player as well and that he felt the split between the Cubs and the hero of their 1929 pennant race was "in the best interests of the club," at least the third time such words had been applied to a Hornsby transaction.[13]

Hornsby was never sure what constituted the final straw that lead to his firing. He tried out different theories with different writers later that year. Occasionally, he proposed the Demaree incident as Veeck's motivation. At other times, he said he thought the president felt Hornsby pinch-hit himself too often: he told Roy Stockton that Veeck had chided him for putting himself "on the spot" in a close game; he complained to Franklin Lane that the people in the Chicago front office "think I'm better on the bench than in the field. If that suits them, it suits me."[14] He also may have thought that Charlie Grimm had campaigned for his dismissal. Because Hornsby tried to acquire Jim Bottomley to play first base in Grimm's place and routinely upbraided Grimm's friends, the easy-going Grimm had grown to despise his manager. Writer Red Smith believed that "what Hornsby thought of Grimm and what Grimm thought of

Hornsby would not make one of the great purple, unforgettable love stories of the ages."[15]

Another angle to his abrupt break with the team hit the newspapers in the middle of August. Cubs players reported to Veeck and then to a few sportswriters that Hornsby had been borrowing money from them to pay his gambling debts; they now doubted that they would get their money back. When the team passed Pittsburgh for first place on August 11, newspapers ran stories about a "gambling ring" in the Cubs clubhouse and speculated that Hornsby was fired because of it. Commissioner Landis announced an investigation, and Veeck insisted that Hornsby and the other players were clean. The decision to remove Hornsby was a baseball matter, not a gambling one. "If he gambled on the horses," Veeck said in a prepared statement, "I knew nothing of it."[16]

Veeck certainly did know of Hornsby's wagering and had helped organize a payment arrangement between the ex-manager and his creditors Woody English, Guy Bush, and Charlie O'Leary before Landis summoned them all to a meeting. Interviewed separately by the commissioner, the Cubs denied involvement in any type of gambling, and Hornsby strongly denied that any of his teammates ever joined him at the track. He further explained that he had borrowed money from his fellow players to make payments on his farm's mortgage and to the Internal Revenue Service, not bookmakers. This was at least partly true. After an audit in 1931, the IRS had decided Hornsby owed more than $8,000 in back taxes for 1926 and 1927. Because he first had to pay the sudden tax debt, Hornsby found himself without cash when he incurred a few large gambling losses and had borrowed money from his teammates to stay even. Veeck repeated the same story to Judge Landis. The commissioner, incredulous but without evidence against the men, let the matter drop with just a warning.

Guided by the softer touch of Charlie Grimm, the Cubs played twenty games better than even on their way to an easy pennant victory. A win over the distant Pirates on September 20 clinched the title, and 150,000 Chicagoans fêted the North Side team with a large parade the next day. A showdown with McCarthy's Yankees loomed in the World Series. The formality of deciding which members of the organization would receive shares in the postseason royalties took place on September 23; perhaps influenced by their minor "gambling" scandal, Hornsby's former players voted that he would not be included. The deposed manager immediately appealed to Judge Landis, claiming he was responsible for several young players' development and had been part of more than half the team's victories. His plea fell on deaf ears at the commissioner's office, though.

Landis had believed Hornsby to be a reprobate gambler and sullying influence on his teammates for years, and his impressions were confirmed during the August inquisition. Hornsby's appeal gave the commissioner an opportunity to censure Hornsby indirectly. Landis almost gleefully announced that he would not overturn the Cubs decision due to the fact that a player had to be on a team's active roster or injured list to receive a postseason share. Hornsby had been a "free agent" for more than a month and thus was not "eligible," but the judge obligingly added that he "would be glad" to hear from Hornsby "in case he knew of any way in which he could be declared a sharer in the players' pool."[17]

Hornsby returned to his farm and had only one conversation with reporters during October—which he initiated—in order to inform the country that he would ignore postseason events and would not even bother to tune in to radio broadcasts of the World Series. "I'm not much concerned about what those fellows are doing up there in New York," he said from his home.[18] He intentionally missed a very lopsided series, as McCarthy's Yankees swept his former teammates in four easy games.

The great hitter did not stay unemployed for very long. Unlike the Wrigley family's Depression-proof chewing gum enterprise, Sam Breadon's automobile sales were declining precipitously. Even though the Cardinals were a strong and successful team, empty seats at Sportsman's Park multiplied as the economy worsened, and Gabby Street's infield had a gap at third base. Breadon believed his old nemesis Hornsby might help address both problems. His fans in St. Louis always remembered the decade's worth of records he achieved there, culminating in the Cardinals first pennant and world championship, and he had remained a celebrity in the city during his peripatetic later career. Breadon dispatched Branch Rickey to the Robertson farm after the World Series to see if Hornsby seemed healthy enough to contribute. The Rajah convinced the general manager that he would be in fine condition by spring, and the men agreed to a $15,000 contract for 1933, contingent on Hornsby's ability to perform.

St. Louisans were pleasantly surprised to hear the news. Hornsby spoke with reporters on October 25, 1932 and swore that he would help his former team win another championship. "I'll hustle every moment for the Cardinals," he promised. "I guess I have slowed up, naturally, as I have grown older, but whatever ability I have left I'll give to the club 100 per cent." Breadon felt compelled to assure the writers that Hornsby's signing was strictly a baseball decision. "I'm not taking this step for sentimental reasons," he said. Hornsby's reputation for unseating his managers was again a topic of discussion, but Gabby Street deflected questions about his job security, allowing that the legendary batter would "be a real help" on the infield and in the dugout. He was quick to add, however, that Hornsby would "have absolutely nothing to say about running the club."[19]

In spring training, the pain from Hornsby's bone spurs had almost completely subsided and he had to fight to get himself in shape. At 37, he was lighter than he had been in two years, and though he had some gray hair and deepening wrinkles around his hazel eyes, Hornsby insisted that he felt like a "rookie" in Bradenton. "I'm more confident than ever that I can help the Cardinals," he announced.[20] Street was pleased with Hornsby's play in exhibition games and confident in his team's chances for the season, but the Rajah's noticeable limp cast doubt on how long his optimistic revival would last.

A different heel problem, soreness in his Achilles tendon, kept him from donning his Redbirds uniform during the first nine games of the regular season, but when he did recuperate enough to play, he was effective but not impressive. He did help the team that year, though, playing second base a few times while Frank Frisch moved to third, and pinch-hitting regularly. His batting average over 83 at-bats was .325, and he hit two balls out of the park, showing that when he felt strong his swing still had real power. Even so, the Cardinals, with and without Hornsby in the lineup, underachieved in the first half of 1933, and appeared to be out of pennant contention by midseason. Sam Breadon, as he often did, grew impatient with his manager.

When his team's record slipped below .500 in mid-July, St. Louis sportswriters knew Gabby Street was doomed. The only question, the experts believed, was who would be his successor. Observers had long thought that Frankie Frisch, the Fordham Flash, had the intelligence and the disposition to make an excellent manager. Since the trade that brought him from New York to St. Louis for Hornsby in 1926, many Cardinals fans expected that the team captain would some day take over as field general. But the Rajah's sudden return to Sportsman's Park, the site of his most successful managerial experience, indicated that Breadon and Rickey would necessarily choose Hornsby to replace Street. It turned out, however, that arrangements had been made for both Hornsby and Frisch to manage in St. Louis.

On July 24, Branch Rickey announced that Frankie Frisch would relieve Street of his duties as manager of the Cardinals. Hornsby, hesitant to encourage another charge of "undermining," claimed he never wanted the job. Of course, he did not need it, because Rickey had arranged another position for him. Though the general manager did not announce it, he released Hornsby the same day he fired Street, and two days later the Rajah cleared National League waivers and signed a three-year contract to play for and manage the St. Louis Browns, presently in last place in the American League.

Philip deCatesby Ball, owner of the Browns for eighteen seasons, was a gruff but likeable man. Like Breadon, he was a self-made millionaire, and like William Wrigley, he took a strong and immediate liking to Hornsby. Ball had forced Bill Killefer, his manager of three years and Hornsby's oldest friend in baseball, to step aside early in July and installed Allen Sothoron, another member of the 1926 champions, as interim manager. Hornsby did not want to take the job from Sothoron and especially hated to appear to supplant Killefer. With Rickey's help, however, Ball convinced Hornsby that he should jump leagues to take on the project of improving the Browns, and the Rajah, charmed by the forthright owner and led by hopes for a secure future, agreed.

Because the Cardinals and the Browns played in the same stadium, they were rarely in St. Louis at the same time, so Hornsby had not seen his new squad in action since the preseason city series. He knew the team was woeful, though. He had a few conversations with Killefer about the players and then met with the press at the announcement of his hiring on July 27. Publicly, he was optimistic. He did not know the team well, he reminded reporters, and before judging his team's chances for improvement he wanted "to have them in hand for some time so that I can familiarize myself with their style of play and what they can do." But, he assured the few remaining Browns' faithful, "I believe I have the nucleus of a good ball club."[21] Afterward, Ball asked him privately if he really believed the Browns could be "great." Hornsby told his new boss bluntly, "It's a lousy ball club, Mr. Ball."[22]

When Hornsby arrived in Chicago to meet the team for a weekend series against the White Sox, he received a summons from Judge Landis. The commissioner invited Hornsby to his offices in the Windy City to offer some advice: the Rajah should stop gambling for the good of the Browns, because more "rumors" about his attention to horseracing would tarnish his new club and baseball as a whole. Since the humiliating "Black Sox" incident which prompted Landis' appointment, Organized Baseball had been relatively free of scandal. An unsubstantiated claim, which arose in 1926, that Tris Speaker and Ty Cobb had conspired to fix games years before and the suspicion of Hornsby's clubhouse "wagering ring" in Chicago had been the only newsworthy examples of gambling interfering with the game. Gambling at the track was not illegal nor was it necessarily related to baseball, but Landis demanded that Hornsby make himself appear above suspicion. His betting on horses must stop. The Rajah spat back that picking races was his form of relaxation and that gambling on horses could not be worse "than it is to gamble on the stock market." He hit a soft spot with the Commissioner when he added, "Like you putting money that belongs to baseball in the stock market and losing." Landis, exasperated by the resolute Hornsby, simply told the Browns manager to go.[23]

The Rajah quickly discovered that his new team was as lousy as he thought. The Browns beat the White Sox in Hornsby's debut game, 3–2, but lost both parts of a double-header the next day by a combined score of 23–9. For the first two weeks of August they won as many games as they lost. Hornsby had yet to put himself into a game, but on August 17 he pinch-hit in the ninth inning against New York. Trailing by a run with a runner on base, "I didn't see anybody on the bench who I thought could hit better than I could, so I grabbed a bat and went to the plate." The Yankees jeered their league's newest player. "So this is the great National League hitter, the great Mr. Hornsby," they shouted. From his famous position in the back corner of the batter's box, he took a youthful cut at Lefty Gomez's first pitch and hit a home run to win the game. Circling the bases as the Yankees walked off the field, he said, "Yes, this is the great National League hitter—still good enough to beat you goddamned sons-of-bitches." His first plate appearance in the American League had bested the great Yankees and produced the two hundred ninety-ninth home run of his career.[24]

That game was the highlight of an uninspiring start to his time with the Browns. Over the next six weeks the team lost twenty-five out of thirty-five games and Hornsby rarely played, accumulating only 9 at-bats. For the season, the Browns had only one player with a batting average over .300 and had two pitchers lose nineteen games. Their record of 55–96 (19–33 under Hornsby) was the worst in baseball. For the Rajah, who had no other prospects to manage and certainly none to play, his position with the Browns was a necessity because he needed his salary more than ever. However, for the first time in his life, he was not looking forward to the next spring.

During the summer of 1933, Hornsby had defaulted on a mortgage payment for his farm. His off-season home had also been an unprofitable business venture for years, especially once depression hit the country. With golf course development necessarily curtailed, sales of the sod Hornsby developed on the farm dropped sharply. Combined with his debts to the IRS and his gambling habit, the farm's losses had become more than his decreased salary could cover. Now earning only $18,000 per season, he had no choice but to auction the farm, which brought him some immediate cash to pay his debts but resulted in a $20,000 net loss. He installed his family in a rented house in a St. Louis neighborhood, but Jeannette was drinking heavily and losing patience with his gambling losses and recurring financial catastrophes. Within a year she would file for divorce, though she never proceeded with the action. Their marriage was not over, but it was crumbling.

In the 1933–1934 offseason, he attempted to recuperate as much money as possible by participating in exhibition games around the Midwest and by coaching, for the second time, at a baseball school in the resort town Hot Springs,

Arkansas. The barnstorming was difficult due to his persistent ankle injuries, but he found that tipping his cap and taking a turn at bat could yield an easy $100 or so. The real stars of those games, however, were the Negro League players like Josh Gibson or Satchel Paige, who showed that they were as good as—and better than—most of the major league players on the field with them. At Ray Doan's baseball school in early February, Hornsby had the pleasure of baseball conversations with his friends Grover Cleveland Alexander and George Sisler as well as a captive audience of aspiring ballplayers. There was little that Hornsby enjoyed more than discussing the fine points of hitting and plate discipline with an interested young man. Though his share of the camp's profits was small, Hornsby repeated his role as chief instructor at Hot Springs for several years.

His new organization also demanded his services in the off-season. On October 22, Phil Ball had died suddenly and left the struggling franchise in the hands of his disinterested estate. Ball had been a charismatic leader of the franchise who respected his employees' efforts and was willing to absorb financial setbacks with his personal fortune. His executors, on the other hand, wanted nothing but to have the organization run itself until a buyer was identified. Hornsby, who felt he had entrusted his future career to Ball personally, and Louis Von Weise were set with the task of reducing the club's debt without regard for the team's performance. Over the two years that the Ball estate held on to the American League team, the pair sold off many of their minor league prospects and traded a few veteran Browns for cheaper players and as much cash as possible. A bad team was mortgaging its future.

Hornsby once explained to writer Franklin Lane that there was "no black art about management." To run a team well a manager had three fundamental requirements: "First, he must have the material. Second, he must get the fellows pulling together. Third, he must develop a system of play that will produce results, and stick to that system."[25] During the seasons of 1934–1937 when he managed the Browns, the Rajah rarely achieved even one of his prerequisites for success. His teams were made up of castoffs and an annual infusion of unpromising rookies; the losing spirit and revolving roster prevented much team unity from developing; and though he stayed firmly to the strategies that had won games for him with the Cardinals, Giants, and Cubs, results were much nearer to those of the 1928 Braves. Watching his team struggle for the better part of four years and working desperately to keep his roster stocked with acceptable talent, Hornsby began to view his managerial duties as a real job rather than as part of a game.

The franchise itself suffered during his tenure as well. Hornsby was caught in a seemingly inescapable cycle of poor field performance and diminishing funds for improvement. Attendance was already on a downward slope when he was hired, but the annual successes of the Cardinals and restrained consumer spending contributed to keep people away from Browns games in record numbers. The National League's "Gashouse Gang" was a polished and entertaining team, while the American League team that played in Sportsman's Park was a jumble of forgettable losers that never seemed to get better. Rollie Hemsley, whom Hornsby brought down from Chicago to catch, was an amusing headache for his manager and also the team's most popular player with fans. However, the Browns had very few fans: they had the lowest number of paying customers in the league every year of the 1930s. They reached their nadir in 1935, when they drew only 80,922 fans, the lowest total attendance figure for any team between the wars.[26] The average of just more than 1,000 fans per game was far less than the Cardinals and also the St. Louis Stars, three-time Negro National League champions, who had begun playing games and paying rent at Sportsman's Park.

Von Weise began to blame Hornsby for both the team's poor performance and the fans' waning interest, but to fire Hornsby would require the cash-strapped team to honor his contract and continue to pay his large salary. After a 57–95 finish in 1936, the club president even consulted with Landis to see if Hornsby's betting might provide a way out for the team, but the commissioner said his hands were tied. The matter was dropped when the team was finally sold to banker Donald Barnes, who replaced Von Weise with Bill DeWitt, a former assistant and disciple of Branch Rickey. Gambling would indeed figure into Hornsby's break with the club as much—if not more—than losing, however.

Just as he had explained to Judge Landis in 1933, the racetrack was the only place Hornsby really found relaxation from the stress of his recent baseball and financial difficulties. He lost often and won occasionally, but kept his gambling debts small enough to appease Jeannette. He kept himself on the team's active roster the entire time he managed, still pinch-hitting when he thought it necessary and filling in at first base a few times. Though he claimed to feel agile enough to be worthy of the roster spot, his detractors believed Hornsby was only aiming to become the sixth man to reach 3,000 career hits. His career total before the '37 season was 2,912, and he had publicly daydreamed about "leaving just a little more behind" for his personal legacy.[27] But he rarely put himself into games, and it seemed unlikely he would get 88 at-bats that year, let alone the necessary hits.

His stress was at a high when the Browns returned to St. Louis after losing fourteen out of sixteen games on the first long road trip of 1937. Browns fans, recovering from the Depression and turning out to see the team again, started clamoring for a change. To compound his managerial frustrations, Hornsby was in debt to his owner. Upon purchase of the club, Barnes had made a sign of faith in the manager by inviting him to invest in the banker's loan enterprise, and then advanced him the money to purchase the stock. By the summer of 1937, Hornsby still owed Barnes $6,000. To maintain the trust of his new boss, who pleased Hornsby by refusing to interfere with his personnel decisions, Hornsby was desperate to erase their debts and reverse their team's fortunes on the field. Naturally, he would address the problems his own way.

After losing eleven out of twelve games at the beginning of July, St. Louis was seventh in the American League, only a game in front of Connie Mack's truly awful Athletics, a franchise that seemed to operate only at the extremes of success. With Boston visiting Sportsman's Park July 14, Hornsby shared a race tip with Red Sox pitcher Bobo Newsom, who had spent the two previous years in the Browns' starting rotation. A three-horse parlay paid off big for Hornsby, who bet with both a St. Louis and a Chicago bookie, and Newsom, pleased to have made a small sum himself, bought a round of drinks after that afternoon's game. One of the men he bought a drink for was Browns' general manager Bill De-Witt.

The following Monday, Hornsby walked into Barnes' office with a cashier's check for $6,000 to settle their debt. DeWitt had already informed Barnes of the windfall, and when Rogers presented the money to the owner, Barnes asked him where he got it. "Where-in-the-hell do you think I got it? I don't remember you making this an extra payday," Hornsby said. The owner refused the check on grounds that he wouldn't accept gambling proceeds as payments. "The money is as good as the money you take from people in the loan-shark business," Hornsby told the banker, leaving the check on his desk. "It's better than taking interest from widows and orphans."[28] Three days later on July 20, after the Browns lost both games of a double-header to the Yankees, DeWitt announced the manager's dismissal.

The rumor of Hornsby's exchange with Barnes quickly spread around the league, but no one involved would confirm that Hornsby had been fired for his impertinence or his gambling. Barnes would only say he made the firing "for cause." When a reporter told the Rajah that someone had hinted that his betting led directly to his dismissal, he waved the story off. "Aw, they always bring that up," he exclaimed. "That's the theme song, so let 'em sing it if they want to."[29]

If Hornsby argued that he was fired for losing, his case did have some merit. The first half of the 1937 season was the worst stretch in Hornsby's time with the Browns, which was largely defined by losing streaks. With a winning percentage of .398 in the American League, his fame and the franchise's general ineptitude were likely the only reasons he had survived in the position long enough to lose more than 350 games. But for a team that could feel no further embarrassment for its incompetence, the smudge of impropriety that Hornsby's excessive wagering put on the organization was the only possible reason to let him go. As his successor Jim Bottomley, the former Cardinal, decided, "If Rajah was fired because we lost two yesterday, I'm liable to go tomorrow."[30]

With one good bet, Rogers Hornsby had effectively ended his major league career. The financial hardships he had suffered during most of the 1930s had been temporarily eased by the winning parlay, but the cost he paid to settle his debts was the life in baseball he loved. Over the next fifteen years, Hornsby would take jobs in and around the game from nearly whoever would pay him, both to cover his family's expenses and to satisfy his passion. Occasionally, such as during a brief turn managing a Mexican League team or when he became part of Chicago Mayor Richard Daley's administration, the tale of "old hard-boiled Hornsby" would surface again in the columns of his sportswriter friends. Within major league baseball, however, the Rajah simply became a legend from the game's storied past.

Hornsby's exploits on the field had scored deep marks in the memory of many around the game. The shove into retirement he received from Donald Barnes in 1937 prompted a few writers to consider what Hornsby had accomplished, and their assessments confirmed that the .358 career hitter had "generally been rated the greatest right-handed batter the National League ever produced" and that many of his records, particularly his 1924 average of .424, would last for ages.[31] His inability to relate with his teammates or with baseball officials had changed the tenor of his great career, however, and John Kieran of the *New York Times* believed the carousel ride in his latter years would be his lasting image. Kieran concluded, "So the record of Hornsby is that they admired him, they went after him, they got him, he did well—and they fired him, one after the other."[32]

NOTES

1. Smith, *Storied Stadiums: Baseball's History Through Its Ballparks*, 129.

2. Ed McCauley column, *Cleveland Plain Dealer* [1952], clipping, Rogers Hornsby Collection, The Sporting News Archives, St. Louis.

3. Sid Keener, "Sid Keener's Column," *St. Louis Star* [1931], clipping, Rogers Hornsby Collection, The Sporting News Archives, St. Louis.

4. "Wilson Suspended for Rest of Season," *New York Times*, September 7, 1931, 9.

5. 1931 Chicago Cubs, BaseballLibrary.com, http://www.baseballlibrary.com/baseballlibrary/teams/1931cubs.stm.

6. "Wilson is Pleased; Censures Hornsby," *New York Times*, December 10, 1931, 31.

7. "Breadon, Here, Predicts Comeback by Wilson," *New York Times*, December 19, 1931, 25.

8. *Sporting News*, February 4, 1932, 2.

9. J. Roy Stockton column, *St. Louis Post-Dispatch* [February 1932], clipping, Rogers Hornsby Collection, The Sporting News Archives, St. Louis.

10. Hornsby, *My Kind of Baseball*, 106.

11. "Hornsby Dropped; Grimm Cubs Pilot," *New York Times*, August 3, 1932, 18.

12. *Chicago Tribune*, August 3, 1932, 1.

13. "Hornsby Dropped; Grimm Cubs Pilot," 18.

14. J. Roy Stockton, Foreword to Hornsby, *My Kind of Baseball*, 20; F. C. Lane, "The Passing of Rogers Hornsby," *Baseball Magazine*, October 1932, 487.

15. "Views of the Sport" column, November 19, 1953, clipping, Rogers Hornsby Collection, The Sporting News Archives, St. Louis.

16. *New York Times*, August 12, 1932, 20.

17. *New York Times*, October 15, 1932, 21.

18. *New York Times*, September 30, 1932, 27.

19. *New York Times*, October 26, 1932, 23.

20. *St. Louis Post-Dispatch*, March 12, 1933, pt. 2, 1.

21. "Hornsby Is Signed to Manage Browns," *New York Times*, July 27, 1933, 22.

22. Daley, "He Who Gets Slapped," 31.

23. Hornsby and Surface, *My War with Baseball*, 25; Broeg, "Mr. Blunt: The One and Only Rogers Hornsby," 25.

24. Hornsby, *My Kind of Baseball*, 119–120.

25. Lane, "The Passing of Rogers Hornsby," 488.

26. Baltimore Orioles Attendance, Stadium and Park Factors, Baseball-Reference. com, http://www.baseball-reference.com/teams/BAL/attend.shtml.

27. Arthur Siegel, "Ambitious Rajah Hoping to Reach 3000-Hit Mark" [March 20, 1936], clipping, Rogers Hornsby Collection, National Baseball Library, Cooperstown, NY.

28. Hornsby and Surface, *My War with Baseball*, 27–28.

29. *St. Louis Post-Dispatch*, July 22, 1937, 1B.

30. *New York Herald*, July 22, 1937, clipping, Rogers Hornsby Collection, National Baseball Library, Cooperstown, NY.

31. Lane, "The Passing of Rogers Hornsby," 488.

32. John Kieran, "Hornsby the Vanishing American," *New York Times*, August 5, 1932, 18.

TO BASEBALL'S
HINTERLANDS AND BACK

In a barbershop on January 20, 1942, Rogers Hornsby, the new manager of the Fort Worth Cats, heard that the BBWAA had voted to name him the twenty-seventh member of National Baseball Hall of Fame. Smiling underneath a foamy layer of shaving cream, he thanked the small group of reporters who had gathered to inform him and sighed, "That's a mighty fine honor."[1] Later, with his graying hair in a neat crew cut, he held a small press conference at LaGrave Field, home of the Cats, and the attending press informed him of the details of his election. Of the 233 voting baseball writers, 182 had put the Rajah on their ballot. It was explained to him that he was the only person selected for the Hall that season. Other luminaries from his playing days like Frank Frisch and Mickey Cochrane, as well as former Cubs Johnny Evers and Frank Chance had not received the three-fourths majority required for induction. Additionally, he had been voted in over his first manager, Miller Huggins. Hornsby, always modest when awarded special attention and definitely always blunt, made a simple statement: "It's quite a distinction, but right now there's a couple things more important: First, winning the war. Second, baseball."[2]

Only six weeks had passed since Japanese bombers had attacked Pearl Harbor, and it had been just two months since he accepted the position with the Cats. On the other hand, his selection for the Hall of Fame, certainly the highest honor available to a baseball player, was not going to be a part of his daily life. The bas-relief plaque with his face and career achievements would hang on the wall in Cooperstown, New York, half a continent away from his office at LaGrave Field. He was in full command of the Texas League organization, and

Hornsby was looking ahead to a spring in which many of his players might be called away to serve their country. The business of baseball's present always took precedence for Hornsby over nostalgia for his playing days.

Some reminiscence was inevitable, though, and the new reminder of the excellence of his past career was likely a bittersweet one for Hornsby. He had anticipated his election into baseball's memorial hall since 1936, when he finished ninth on the initial ballot by the sportswriters association, with about 100 votes less than Ty Cobb and Babe Ruth, whose selections were nearly unanimous. To be ranked so highly while he was still on an active roster struck him as a mark of tremendous respect and, after the rule was added that a player's career must be over for at least five years to be considered, Hornsby had looked forward to joining his great peers at Cooperstown. Of course, he expected to be a part of major league baseball when that time came.

In 1938, when Rogers Hornsby agreed to manage the Chattanooga Lookouts, a higher-level minor league team, reporters asked him if his combination of bright prospects and ex-big leaguers could win. It was a question Hornsby was used to answering as a manager, and he casually replied that there was nothing to do but "play your cards and see what happens."[3] After his firing by Donald Barnes, the Rajah had executed his professional life with that same philosophy: taking jobs wherever he could find them in baseball, bringing his eagerness to win and his long experience in the game, and leaving as soon as he or his employers felt it necessary. J. G. Taylor Spink would describe the fifteen years between Hornsby's dismissal in St. Louis and his next chance to run a major league team as a "long period of wandering for Rajah in the hinterlands of baseball."[4] He managed or coached with at least a dozen teams at various levels, ranging from semipro exhibition squads to the Pacific Coast League. His new career track took him through Denver, Minneapolis, Baltimore, Chattanooga, Oklahoma City, Fort Worth, Mexico City, Chicago, Beaumont, San Juan, and Seattle. Even considering his sometimes grating personality, the constant switching from organization to organization that defined his life almost as much as his hitting is remarkable. For a man whose best-known activities away from the field were sleeping, sitting in hotel lobbies, and eating steak, he truly got around.

Hornsby's pursuit of a major league manager's position was tireless, but his efforts were fruitless. Immediately after his release from the Browns, he had actually approached Kenesaw Landis in the hope that the commissioner would have suggestions for a job. At the main offices of Organized Baseball in Chicago, Judge Landis stood him up for a scheduled meeting. Hornsby was irate and complained loudly about the commissioner for many years afterward. He believed, correctly, that Landis distrusted him because of his persistent gambling and, though it is unverifiable, that the judge acted directly or indirectly to keep him out of the game.

More than twenty-two seasons since he had last participated in a "bush league" game, Hornsby reacquainted himself with minor league baseball. With admirers who owned the Baltimore Orioles (then a member of the Class AA International League), he quickly got a token position as a hitting instructor and ballpark attraction. Over the next few seasons, as he managed the Orioles, the Lookouts, and the Oklahoma City Indians, he learned that the financial hardships he had faced with the Browns were larger but no more severe than the struggles of most minor league teams. Each of his teams was still attempting to operate independently, without affiliation to a major league club, and tight budgets were the main result of the effort. He also learned about the sideshow tradition in the farm leagues, as he witnessed but refused to participate in skits, races, and other entertainments between innings. In Chattanooga, owner Joe Engel, who was known for the outrageous ballpark stunts he imagined, once stopped a game and presented Hornsby with a mule, intended to poke fun at his infamous addiction to horseracing.[5] Across the leagues as well, clubs regularly announced a "Rogers Hornsby Day" on his first visit to a stadium to capitalize on his name, showering the celebrity manager of the opposing team with gifts while their ticket sales spiked.

He believed that the job he took in his beloved hometown of Fort Worth might become a permanent spot to stay until his next big league opportunity. Hornsby had resigned from his post in Oklahoma City in 1941 because the team could not afford to pay him, but working at LaGrave Field he was paid $9,000 per season plus a share of profits, the largest salary he had received since St. Louis. He was also happy that the oil-rich new owner of the Cats, Stanley Thomspon, had given him full control of the team; finally, he could operate without the supervision of the front office "second-guessers" that he so resented.[6] As general manager, manager, and—on one occasion—second baseman, the new Hall-of-Famer succeeding in pulling the Cats from the bottom of their league to a respectable third place finish in 1942. But teams had lost a number of players to military duty and the other owners decided that, despite the steady economy, the Texas League would shut down for the war's duration.

Unemployed again, the Rajah started to feel desperate. He had no real money and very few assets. Without investments in stocks or real estate left to liquidate, drawing a salary was a necessity. Both his sons were now grown and serving in the military, so he had only himself and Jeannette to support, but no position with even a modest wage was available to him in baseball at the time. "I don't know any other business and I don't want to," he said upon his next hiring. "There's no place left for me in the game here. United States baseball has forgotten me."[7]

A new opportunity and a $1,500 per month salary awaited Hornsby outside the reaches of American baseball. In 1944, an enterprising liquor baron named Jorge Pasquel was attempting to build the poor *Liga Mexicana* into an international attraction by improving the league's standard of play and promoting his league north of the border. He made an aggressive push for recognizable American stars, and Hornsby was his first serious acquisition. Although no other notable major leaguers joined the circuit, Pasquel lured a few draft-exempt prospects away from the farm systems. The finest players he brought to the six-team league were from the Negro Leagues. With promises of $500 monthly paychecks, players such as Theolic Smith, Ferris McDuffie, and Quincey Trouppe headed south and constituted the core talent on teams filled out with inexpensive Cuban and Mexican players.

Hornsby was paid to manage Pasquel's Vera Cruz Blues (the team was named after Pasquel's hometown but actually played in Mexico City). His team, which included another Negro League standout, Ray Dandridge, had only four English speakers besides himself, which limited the instruction he could provide. However, he was enjoying the food, the sunny days, and the relatively competitive—though very high scoring—games, and he took managing with hand signals as a challenge. The long, hot bus rides were tedious, but games were only played in three-game weekend series, so that crowds would be more dense and each contest more profitable for Pasquel, who, besides owning the Blues, also held a stake in each of the other teams.

The Rajah lasted nine games in Mexico. On Saturday, March 31, Hornsby was coaching at third base in the bottom of the ninth inning. His team had won the first game of their third series on Thursday night, and were trailing in the second game 14–13. Word came from the stands that Pasquel wanted Hornsby to pinch-hit. Curious to try out his swing, the manager obliged him. With the bases loaded, "I got hold of one" for a grand slam, he told John Carmichael back in the States. "The air is pretty thin down there and the ball carries." The excited "peons"—as he described the peasant fans—rushed from the stands, "carried me off the field and threw fruit at the other team." The next morning, Pasquel was ambivalent about the victory. "That was a very nice hit yesterday," he told his manager, "but it would have been better if we hadn't won the game." He reasoned that if Vera Cruz had lost, "a big crowd would have come out today to see the deciding game."[8] Hornsby resigned on the spot; he managed the team that afternoon in front of a fairly large audience, then returned to the U.S. having received just one paycheck for his work in Mexico. The Vera Cruz Blues were the last team the Rajah would manage for more than six years.

Watching season after season pass by without an offer of full-time employment, the "stormy petrel" mellowed to become a quiet observer of the sport. Occasionally, he met with individual major leaguers to help solve prolonged slumps, and sometimes managers such as Leo Durocher or Casey Stengel asked him to make a scouting trip. After his return from Mexico, he spent a short time making regular radio broadcasts on WTMV in East St. Louis, Illinois, analyzing games. For the most part, however, Hornsby stayed away from Organized Baseball and kept his ideas and complaints about the game to himself. A reporter checking up on the Rajah for a *Sport* magazine feature story ten years after his last major league game found him surprisingly reserved. "Hornsby, whose career was a crazy-quilt of emotional dynamite, unveils in person none of the spirit of the life he led. His speech is always calm and his opinions, for the most part, are far from violent."9

Without teams of men to direct in the later part of the 1940s, Hornsby focused on his lifelong pleasure of teaching baseball to young people. During that time, his primary employment was as head of the *Chicago Daily News* Baseball Clinics, a series of afternoon camps the newspaper sponsored in neighborhood parks across the city. For $6,000 annually, he provided lessons in the fundamentals of the sport and signed thousands of autographs, a courtesy to children he never denied. The Rajah took a special glee in watching the young Chicagoans practice their skills and challenge each other to games, which reminded him of his sandlot days in Fort Worth.

Hornsby had also always enjoyed his springs in Arkansas as chief instructor at Ray Doan's baseball school, so much so that after Doan withdrew he had continued to operate the barely profitable camp at Hot Springs until 1942. Further, he commented to friends that the most gratifying element of his minor league work was watching young players develop. Although he would rail against major league teams giving large bonuses to unproven high school prospects until the end of his life, a promising 18-year-old was Hornsby's favorite companion in a quiet hotel lobby. Most of his advice centered around proper plate discipline and the virtues of a level swing, but an opportunity to review even the most obscure game situation with a curious youth was never wasted.

The prospect he most loved to teach was his son Bill. Unlike his older half-brother, who had become a career pilot in the U.S. Air Force, William Pennington Hornsby had decided to follow in his famous father's footsteps. After making his own slow exit from the playing field during the 1930s, it had become the Rajah's great wish that his son would keep the Hornsby name alive in major league baseball. According to Jeannette, it was the one thing he always had "his heart set on." When the family was together, Rogers did not "talk about it a great deal, but it [was] there."10 After World War II, Bill did receive a few major league auditions, with the Indians and the White Sox, on the strength of his historic name, but never earned a spot on a regular season roster, although he stayed active in minor league baseball for several years. With 21-year-old Bill's help, however, the Rajah reopened the Rogers Hornsby Baseball School at Hot Springs in 1947, and father and son were able to spend at least one month each spring together on a baseball field for several years.

His son became even more important to Hornsby when faded love and tragedy left Bill as the only immediate family member remaining in his life. Beginning as early as 1932, Jeannette Hornsby had occasionally felt dissatisfied with her marriage, and even temporarily filed for divorce at one point. However, after Jeannette accompanied her husband on a barnstorming tour of Mexico in 1935, the pair returned to a peaceful domestic life for several years. But as Hornsby's career became more unpredictable, Jeannette had taken to heavy drinking, a stark contrast to Rogers' complete abstinence. Then, having lived apart from one another on and off since his month in Mexico in 1944, Rogers and Jeannette permanently separated in 1945. She would formally divorce him in 1952.

The great ballplayer's long estrangement from Rogers Jr. had ended briefly on a trip to California in 1942, but their relationship evaporated while his son moved around the country with the Air Force after World War II. Hornsby heard little from or about his namesake until a few days before Christmas in 1949, when he heard of his son's accidental death. While flying out of Savannah, Georgia on a routine exercise, the younger Rogers' plane crashed into the swampy coastal plain of South Carolina. Hornsby's first son, a father of two children himself, was dead at 29 years old. Hornsby, awe-struck and saddened but unsure of his place, called to offer condolences to his ex-wife Sarah, who refused to allow him to attend the funeral.[11]

Then, in January 1950, a popular former catcher and minor league manager named Chick Autry died suddenly of a heart attack in Savannah. "Those sensitive to human irony," Hornsby biographer Charles Alexander comments, "might have noted that Autry died within a few miles of the spot where Rogers Hornsby Jr. was killed a month earlier, and that Autry's death finally created an opening for the return to Organized Baseball of Rogers Hornsby, Sr."[12] Indeed, just two days after Autry's death, the Rajah was back in the game, replacing the late Autry as manager of the Beaumont Roughnecks.

Seven years after he last managed a team in the United States, Hornsby returned to his usual pattern and managed two different teams in the next two seasons. In the 1950 Texas League, he was praised for reversing the Roughnecks' direction and leading them to their first championship since before World War II. He promptly turned his success into another position, as pilot of the Seattle Rainiers in the more prestigious Pacific Coast League. Hornsby continued his hot streak out west, leading the talented Seattle team to the pennant. He was helped by an MVP season from a 30-year-old rookie named Jim Rivera, whom

Hornsby had seen play in Puerto Rico during the winter and quickly signed for the Rainiers.

Back with an active role in the game he loved, Hornsby managed the two minor league teams with the same notorious zest and bile that contributed to his long absence. A Seattle writer observed him in 1951 as "rather a mysterious loner who is tactless but sincere, patient with clumsy rookies afield but contemptuous when they don't also sleep, talk and live baseball 24 hours a day."[13] Although many considered his hard edge old-fashioned, his recent winning ways also raised the possibility that he would get his long-awaited chance at managing in the big leagues again. Only his lack of "diplomacy" was a reason to doubt that a franchise would consider him. "Baseball men know that Hornsby has one of the keenest minds in the game today. That he isn't still managing a major league club, or possibly sitting in the front office of some club, is something that many people can't understand," James Crusinberry wrote in May 1951.[14] Within months, a long sojourn in baseball's hinterlands would finally come to end for Hornsby; his return to baseball's main stage, however, would be almost comically brief. His performance as he was fired from his first major league post in almost fifteen years—after just fifty-one games—would reveal why the "keen" baseball mind had been absent from the major leagues for so long.

"Hail the Prodigal Rajah!" read a headline announcing Rogers Hornsby's return to the St. Louis Browns.[15] William Veeck Jr., baseball's most notorious showman and son of Hornsby's former boss with the Chicago Cubs, hired Hornsby in October 1951 to manage the St. Louis Browns in the next American League season. Fifteen years after he had been fired in his first term as the team's manager, Rogers Hornsby was returning to the American League through the same door by which he had left it. St. Louis was hardly the same organization that it had been during the Depression, however, and Hornsby's new boss was certainly nothing like Donald Barnes. Nonetheless, there were notable similarities between the 1937 Browns and the 1952 Browns, and they were easy to notice, namely their lack of money, their lack of talent, and their place near the bottom of the junior circuit.

Bill Veeck was making an effort to remedy the situation. Known primarily for the outlandish promotional concepts he brought to the uptight American League rather than the pennant-winning team he had built as president of the Cleveland Indians, Veeck had a well-earned reputation for tomfoolery even before he raised the money to buy the St. Louis team at seven dollars per share in the summer of 1951. His efforts to rejuvenate the city's interest in the team that year were unorthodox and widely reported, cementing his status as the game's most outrageous personality.

The most exciting idea—and the most quickly vetoed by American League president William Harridge—was the new owner's plan to pick a manager-for-a-day via a newspaper contest. If the Browns were going to lose, he said, their fans may at least have a say in how they did it. After his proposed sweepstakes was shot down by the league office, Veeck had kept his next concept close to his vest. Then, on August 19, 1951, during a game against the Detroit Tigers at Sportsman's Park, he had manager Zach Taylor send the team's most recent roster addition to the plate. Wearing the number "1/8," three-feet seven-inches tall Eddie Gaedel settled into a stance that created a two-inch strike zone—Gaedel walked on four pitches. Taylor immediately sent in a pinch-runner for the 65-pound Gaedel, who trotted back to the dugout after what would be his only major league appearance. Veeck's stunt drew attention from baseball fans and curiosity seekers around the world. His secret weapon was immediately banned from games by Harridge, who only added to the commotion when he tried to have the midget's name removed for the game's official record.

In a candid moment just after he bought the club, Veeck had sounded pessimistic while discussing the task of hiring a good skipper for his new team. "It may not be easy to find one," he said. "You'd be surprised at how many people there are who don't exactly believe that managing the Browns could be construed as an advancement."[16] But he and Hornsby, it was later revealed, were already discussing the details of a $40,000 contract as early as August. If his hiring of the St. Louis legend was intended as another ploy for publicity, it was successful, because comments on the "most unusual partnership" of owner and manager appeared in every sports column across the country. Roy Stockton wondered aloud in the *Post-Dispatch* about the potential conflicts of Hornsby's "deadly seriousness" with "a laughing man who likes a lot of laughs with his baseball."[17] Veeck, however, had promised there would be "no clowns on the Browns" during the Rajah's tenure, and especially pleased his new manager by agreeing to obtain Jim Rivera's contract from the White Sox, who had just signed the Seattle sensation. Hornsby told Stockton that he looked forward to winning with Veeck: "You know he isn't going to sit still and have a lot of humpty dumpties playing ball for us."[18]

The fanfare for the Rajah's return to Organized Baseball subsided when spring training started at El Centro, California, and the difficult business of creating a winner bogged him down. Although Veeck had tried his best to rejuvenate the team by adding eighteen new faces to the roster, including a trade with the Yankees for outfielder Clint Courtney, most of Hornsby's new Browns were from the mold of the castoffs he had managed for St. Louis during the Depression. Marty Marion, Ned Garver, and Dick Kryhoski were able team leaders and affable men, but after Hornsby installed his former practice regimen and constantly sniped at their deficiencies, they and their fellow Browns immediately lost their taste for the manager.

The players were a generation younger than the 55-year-old former star. Without distinct memories of his 1924 run or his tag on Babe Ruth at the end of the 1926 World Series, their impression of Hornsby shifted quickly from curmudgeonly Hall-of-Famer to obsolete crank. From his contrasting view, he confirmed his beliefs that major leaguers had been pampered since the war era with excessive salaries and permissive clubhouse rules. Therefore, almost from their start together, the skipper and his charges developed a mutual animosity that would never get the chance to subside. With the exception of Jim Rivera and a few other devotees, the Browns started their first season under Hornsby already itching for change.

Bill Veeck also quickly sensed the dissatisfaction of his players. "Open Neck" Veeck, so called because of his customary sport shirts, was a friendly boss who mostly wanted his players to like him. When a massive team slump abruptly halted the Browns' surprising regular season start, players began complaining to him about Hornsby's blatant disregard for their feelings and ideas. He absorbed their criticisms with growing frustration toward his manager.

Browns' pitcher Satchel Paige, the forty-something Negro League idol whom Veeck had signed during spring training with Hornsby's blessing, came to the owner to ask for his release. He wanted to return to his barnstorming All-Star team because, "The manager and me, we don't hit it off." Veeck, a strong advocate of baseball's integration, said he didn't believe Hornsby would let race affect his management of the team and asked Paige if Hornsby singled him out as the team's only black player. No, Paige didn't think so. In fact, he said, "He treats Garver and Kryhoski worse than he does me."[19]

The owner, who was simultaneously discovering that Hornsby's presence had only a minimal effect on ticket sales, decided that the Rajah was through as manager if he made one further provocation. On June 8 at Yankee Stadium, with the Browns in seventh place, the inevitable happened. Hornsby chose not to argue with an umpire's call of fan interference that went against the Browns. Veeck, listening on the radio in St. Louis, actually called New York and sent word to Hornsby in the dugout demanding that his manager issue a formal protest. With the request coming too late and from too far away, Hornsby practically ignored the command.

In Boston two days later, Marty Marion was St. Louis's new manager. A reporter found Hornsby outside the team's hotel, preparing to leave town, and asked for the scoop on the transition. "You can say I was fired or quit," Hornsby replied, clearly agitated. "I don't care."[20] The *Washington Post* asked an unidentified player how he felt about the news and was told, "Well, I got up with a headache this morning and now it's disappeared. Figure out for yourself how I feel about it."[21] Later that afternoon in the visitors' locker room at Fenway Park, the Browns, freed of their hated taskmaster, presented Veeck with a 3-foot trophy engraved with the inscription, "To Bill Veeck: For the greatest play since the Emancipation Proclamation."[22]

NOTES

1. *Sporting News*, January 29, 1942, 2.
2. "Hornsby Is Appreciative," *New York Times*, January 21, 1942, 25.
3. *Sporting News*, July 7, 1938, 5.
4. Spink, "The Strange Story of Rogers Hornsby," 5.
5. Hornsby and Surface, *My War with Baseball*, 97–98.
6. *St. Louis Post-Dispatch*, January 14, 1933, 15.
7. Alexander, *Rogers Hornsby*, 231.
8. *Chicago Daily News*, May 25, 1944, 28.
9. Sher, "Rogers Hornsby: The Mighty Rajah," 58.
10. Ibid., 60.
11. Alexander, *Rogers Hornsby*, 239.
12. Ibid., 240.
13. Al Wolf, "Sportraits," clipping, Rogers Hornsby Collection, The Sporting News Archives, St. Louis.
14. James Crusinberry, "Rogers Hornsby, Non-Stop Man of Baseball," *Baseball Magazine*, May 1951, 409–410.
15. Frank Graham, "Hail the Prodigal Rajah!" *Sport*, May 1952, 20ff.
16. *Sporting News*, August 4, 1951, 2.
17. *Sporting News*, October 17, 1951, 5.
18. Ibid.
19. Milton Gross column [June 1952], clipping, Rogers Hornsby Collection, The Sporting News Archives, St. Louis.
20. *Sporting News*, June 18, 1952, 1.
21. "Quotes: The Rajah's Gone—But Not Forgotten," June 25, 1952, clipping, Rogers Hornsby Collection, The Sporting News Archives, St. Louis.
22. "Now It Can Be Told: Veeck Bought Own Loving Cup" [June 1952], clipping, Rogers Hornsby Collection, National Baseball Library, Cooperstown, NY.

HORNSBY'S BEND

Hornsby's long-time friend Grover Cleveland Alexander died on November 4, 1950, as a fairly penniless and incorrigibly alcoholic man, bitter with the way he had been treated by Organized Baseball, which had refused him a pension. Just after Bill Veeck fired him from the Browns, Hornsby was thinking of his late friend's fate and remembered the statement Pete had given when released from his final team. "I've given more to baseball than it's given me," the great right-hander had said. "I've never been a 'goody-goody' boy, but I stayed in there and pitched."[1]

The Rajah felt much the same way throughout his career. He had a true passion for his sport, perhaps too extreme for his own good, that compelled him to rush out onto a baseball field each spring. He wanted to be paid for his talents, but his enjoyment of the game was primary to him. Unfortunately, his dedication to an ideal form of baseball and subsequent deafness to the suggestions of those around him led to a career-long cycle of feuds with teammates and breaks with ownership. After he was fired by Bill Veeck in 1952, Hornsby felt disenfranchised from the game he had made his life. Even so, over the course of his life's final decade, Hornsby returned to the diamond each year, pitching his version of baseball to anyone who would listen.

Hornsby did have another opportunity to manage in the major leagues after leaving St. Louis. Almost immediately after his dismissal, in fact, Luke Sewell stepped down from his job as skipper of the Cincinnati Reds, who were in last place at the start of August 1952. General Manager Gabe Paul, a baseball traditionalist and hence Veeck's opposite, signed the Rajah on the theory that, in

Hornsby, after his major league managing career ended, turned his attention to teaching baseball to the youth of Chicago for several years in the 1950s. *National Baseball Hall of Fame Library, Cooperstown, N.Y.*

order to have been fired on so many occasions, he must have been good enough to be hired so often. His position with the Reds would end up as the last opportunity to run a team; though his tenure with the franchise was brief, it proved to be the most peaceful of his career.

At the time he accepted Paul's offer, rumors that Veeck had purchased the "Emancipation Proclamation" trophy for himself as another publicity stunt were slowing being corroborated, and the Rajah's ire was permanently inflamed. Carefully excluding Jim Rivera and Clint Courtney, who had remained loyal to him, Hornsby regularly slammed the Browns and their owner in the press. With his temper and candid tongue directed elsewhere, he managed another bad team to a slight improvement and his new players believed that the Rajah "made sense."[2] Impatient Reds fans, however, coerced Paul to make another change before the end of the 1953 season because Cincinnati failed to climb in the standings. With sarcastic humor, Hornsby agreed that "when this happens the thing to do is change managers since they get all the blame for losing."[3]

With his Cincinnati job finished, Hornsby returned to the apartment building on Chicago's North Side he had purchased with his redundant 1952 and 1953 salaries from his Browns' and Reds' contracts, ready to relax before organizing the Rogers Hornsby Baseball School set for the upcoming February. A personal tragedy awaited him, however. Bernadette Harris, his companion since separating from Jeannette a few years before, had been suffering from severe depression for some time. Recently, she had lived with him during the season near Cincinnati, but she left for their Chicago apartment ahead of Hornsby as he settled his affairs with the Reds. On Labor Day of 1953, she leapt from a window on the third floor of Hornsby's property. With his divorce from Jeannette not yet settled, Rogers had always referred to Bernadette as "my good friend and secretary," but she had at times called herself Mrs. Hornsby. When police found a card in her purse that instructed, "In case of accident notify Rogers Hornsby," her "employer" was called to the inquest into her death.[4] Cleared of responsibility, Hornsby never spoke of Harris' death in public again. Therefore, the depth of his grief is difficult to measure. Within a few years, however, he would meet and then marry a woman named Marjorie Porter, whose strong Christian faith seemed to provide her the fortitude required to live with the moody and occasionally viciously mean former baseball star.

For the duration of the 1950s, Hornsby remained employed in the city of Chicago, and began to refer to the city as his home, completing his life's northern migration through the Midwest from Fort Worth to St. Louis to Chicago. Reprising his role as head of the *Daily News* clinics under the auspices of Mayor Richard Daley's Youth Foundation, Hornsby taught baseball to children in his adopted city for four years. As long as he lived, Hornsby would remark that his hours with the kids in the city parks were some of the most fun experiences of his life. Living within walking distance of Wrigley Field also allowed the Rajah to satisfy his addiction to baseball in the major leagues, and the Cubs eventually hired their former manager as a batting instructor for spring training and in-season consultations.

His professional career ended with a franchise that was just beginning—a mark, perhaps, that a new era in baseball had arrived. In 1961 he was hired as a scout for the New York Metropolitans, an expansion team set to begin play the next year, and the team assigned him to scour the Chicago area for prospects to fill their farm system. The next spring, his friend Casey Stengel, former leader of the Yankees and the man charged with managing the nascent franchise's inaugural season, invited the Rajah to don a uniform again. Hornsby, almost a decade removed from his season with the Reds, was by now content with the prospect that he would never manage again. He happily agreed to join Stengel in the Shea Stadium dugout, though he knew the Mets were by far the worst team with which he ever aligned himself. With his short, gray hair hidden under his royal blue cap, and his dimples piercing his softening cheeks, Hornsby rattled off the accumulated advice of more than forty years in professional baseball to players like Marv Throneberry and Charlie Neal. The 40–120 campaign, a record that at another time in his life might nearly have killed Hornsby, was one of the most carefree seasons of his baseball life.

Hornsby believed his eyes were his greatest asset as a professional ballplayer, and so he protected them feverishly throughout his life. Shunning any recreational reading and avoiding the flickering lights of movie theaters, he managed to maintain one of the sharpest set of eyes in baseball. However, complications with his eyes—and quite possibly his lifelong diet of red meat—ultimately led to his death. After his season with the Mets was finished, Hornsby arranged to have a cataract that had developed over one of his eyes treated. On December 10, the cataract was removed, but he did not recover from the surgery well. Within four days, he had a stroke, and he remained hospitalized through the holiday season. His condition appeared to improve, but on the morning of January 5, 1963, Hornsby's heart stopped. A myocardial infarction, which blocked the supply of blood to the heart muscles, had spurred a small heart attack the evening before, and, by morning, he suffered complete cardiac failure.[5]

His wife Marjorie and his stepdaughter Mary Beth were at his side when he died at Wesley Memorial Hospital in Chicago. They made arrangements for a memorial service in their home city and to travel with Hornsby's body for his burial in Texas. Mary Beth made a short statement to reporters that reflected the unpretentious but direct manner of the late Hall-of-Famer. "He didn't like flowers and his desire was that none be sent," she said. "He wanted any such money to go to the National Heart Fund instead."[6]

Rogers Hornsby's grave at his family cemetery in Hornsby's Bend, Texas is marked with a low, white marble headstone that reads, in a plain font, "Rogers Hornsby, April 27, 1896–January 5, 1963." The simple flourish chosen to commemorate those years is a generic symbol of the game he loved: two baseball bats crossed beneath a ball. A journalist visiting the memorial park near the turn in the Colorado River found it to be "a peaceful spot, euphoric, far from any mechanization. The whisper of wind mingles only with the cheery hum of insects and birds."[7] For the man who most wanted simply to hit, to win, and then to be let alone, the setting seems to be a fitting site for his permanent rest.

At the funeral service, hundreds of Hornsbys, from his most distant relatives to his brother Everett and his sister Margaret as well as his son Bill, came to their ancestral home to honor the most famous member of their family since its patriarch Reuben. They were joined by many of the 105 honorary pallbearers, a group which included umpires, former players, and sportswriters, along with lifelong friends; their number and attendance showed that the man reporters appreciatively came to call "Mr. Blunt," who so effectively alienated many of his peers during his life, had been kind in his honesty often enough to win and keep friends. Interred in his modest gravesite, in the same patch of long green grass as his parents and two brothers, the mighty Rajah was returned to his roots. At home in his beloved Texas, Rogers Hornsby could be remembered as the person he had wanted to be—a modest, honest man who made a simple living playing the game he loved.

NOTES

1. "Alexander Faces Baseball Oblivion" [June 1930], clipping, Grover Cleveland Alexander Collection, National Baseball Library, Cooperstown, NY.

2. Tom Swope, "Rog Lays It on Line for Reds; They Agree He 'Makes Sense,' " *Sporting News*, August 13, 1952, 21.

3. Hornsby and Surface, *My War with Baseball*, 54.

4. "Hornsby at Plunge Inquest," *Chicago Tribune*, September 8, 1953, Rogers Hornsby Collection, The Sporting News Archives, St. Louis.

5. *Chicago Daily News*, January 7, 1963; Alexander, *Rogers Hornsby*, 302.

6. Alexander, *Rogers Hornsby*, 302.

7. John Husar, "In Texas History, Reuben Hornsby Outranks Rog," *Sporting News*, January 14, 1978, 42.

MAKING OF A LEGEND

"Even by the generous standards of major-league baseball, a business notorious for its high percentage of primitives and mavericks, the late Rogers Hornsby was the bench mark by which intransigence had to be measured," wrote Bill Surface in the *Saturday Evening Post* six months after the ballplayer's death. "He was a tangle of contradictions so exasperating and sometimes so astonishing that the best that could be done was to *appreciate* him."[1] Surface, who had co-authored Hornsby's second autobiography, *My War with Baseball*, clearly wrote from a position of exasperation in his article, "The Last Days of Rogers Hornsby," but many of the other baseball writers who eulogized Mr. Blunt in 1963 truly also seemed to appreciate the many faults and idiosyncrasies of the player whose talents were never disputed. Bob Broeg and his sportswriter pals teasingly called the Hall-of-Famer "Old Sweet Talk" and acknowledged that Hornsby "must have thought that diplomacy was a respiratory disease," but to them the sharp tongue and brusque manner humanized one of baseball's largest personalities.[2] Through the more than four decades that have passed since Hornsby last pulled a cap over his crew-cut white hair, these dual perspectives on the Rajah have shaped his legacy. His achievements as a player are recognized as among the most remarkable in baseball history; several of them, such as his .424 batting average in 1924, few would expect to see repeated. However, depending upon the observer, Hornsby's personal manner is remembered alternately as independent and dedicated to his chosen profession or as belligerent, ignorant, and self-serving.

"The Last Days of Rogers Hornsby" is probably the most important and most polarizing comment on the player that appeared after his death. The publication of Surface's article drew ire from many of Hornsby's family, friends, and fans, not for reiterating the man's curmudgeonly ways or well-known "compulsion for slow horses," but because the writer portrayed Hornsby as guilty of particular prejudices and a deepening disregard for the sport he loved.[3] Surface may have been in a unique position to evaluate the Rajah's final years, given that the two worked together for about eighteen months writing two articles and the book that would be Hornsby's last statement on his career and of his opinions on the modern form of baseball. Surface reports that Hornsby was not only addicted to gambling but preoccupied with it. In Surface's account, the man whose passion for talking baseball was legendary is uninterested in their project and values his co-author for his facility with the racing form rather than with his pen. When the writer does recount their baseball conversations, Hornsby's most memorable pronouncements are that any able-bodied boy who chooses not to play the game "ain't an American" and that he would "beat the hell out of" Ernie Banks, literally, if he were the Cubs manager. "That guy'd be in the local city hospital getting sewed up," the 65-year-old Chicago resident had said of Banks, dismissing the star shortstop as too "nonchalant" and "easygoing."[4]

Surface perceived Hornsby as engaged in a perpetual "liturgy of hatred." The native Texan was certainly a man of deep convictions, and he often gave the appearance of narrow-mindedness. "His apparent prejudices against Jews and Negroes were shocking," the writer commented, "but, on examination, turned out to be simply two items in a long accounting against the world."[5] By all accounts, Hornsby was slow to give acceptance to any person, regardless of race or creed, but Surface's charges of overt bigotry brought friends and observers to the late player's defense.

Zeke Handler, who knew Hornsby since both were boys in Fort Worth, dashed off a letter to the *Sporting News* immediately after reading the *Saturday Evening Post* article. "I counted myself among the few people the great Cardinal star of the 1920s considered his 'friends,'" he wrote, "and I am of full Hebraic extraction." Hornsby, he pointed out, had customarily attached "a few choice expletives" to the word "Jew" when Handler peeved him, but an accusation of anti-Semitism was unfounded because Hornsby had spent countless hours in the company of several Jewish men, none of whom ever felt he discriminated against them.[6]

Countering allegations of Hornsby's racial prejudices was more difficult. Hornsby was hardly an outspoken advocate of desegregation and rarely went out of his way to acknowledge the talents of African American players. When his old associate Branch Rickey signed Jackie Robinson for the Brooklyn Dodgers in 1945, the *Brooklyn Eagle* quoted Hornsby's thoughts on the subject. "It won't work out," he opined, because "ball players on the road live much closer together." He continued—either diffusing the idea that white players would be prejudiced against a black teammate or criticizing the adaptability of crossovers from the Negro Leagues—"It will be more difficult for the Negro to adjust himself to the life of the major league club, than for the white players to accept him."[7]

In a book published almost fifteen years after Hornsby's death, sportswriter Fred Lieb revealed that Hornsby, as well as Gabby Street and Tris Speaker, had individually revealed to him that "they were members of the Ku Klux Klan."[8] Although this was probably factual—and not a point of pride—Hornsby biographer Charles Alexander, who is also a historian of the Klan, notes that the Rajah's participation was at most "semiactive." According to Alexander, prominent men from southern states were practically conscripted into the Klan as it made a push to become a legitimate social organization, but, by the late 1920s, the group lost a significant portion of its membership, including Hornsby, to attrition.[9] So it seems to one authority that if the Texas native had been part of the Klan, he was never a white-hooded cross-burner, but rather just an impressive name on the register.

This is not to say that Hornsby was not capable of racism. The Texan used racial epithets as freely as anyone at the time, and on occasion refused to participate in barnstorming games that included African Americans. He did, however, play willingly against Negro League stars at other times, including a significant 1935 "All-Star" series in Mexico City, and, by the end of his career, he regularly coached black players. Ultimately, the case seems to be as Surface implied it was: Hornsby's tactlessness and discrimination against players was symptomatic of a general lack of connection with a host of different types of people. He was unimpressed by and rude to a large portion of his acquaintances; African American or Jewish players comprised only a subset of those Hornsby grievously offended in his lifetime. Hornsby respected men who respected baseball, and it was the slightest sign of disloyalty to the sport that caused him to dislike individual players.

The game and its players had changed dramatically during Hornsby's lifetime, due in part to the change in American culture after World War II, and in part to the development of playing and training technologies. Hornsby was definitely unsettled by many of the changes, primarily what he saw as the transfer of authority from the field managers to the front offices, which pursued publicity rather than wins. However, he had publicly defended the state of the sport on several occasions, including a journalistic debate with Ty Cobb. In 1952, the former Tiger published an article in *Life* called "They Don't Play Baseball Any More" (which, incidentally, excluded Hornsby from a list of history's greatest players). Hornsby, preparing to return as manager of the Browns and perhaps hungry for the publicity of a minor controversy, wrote a response in *Look* magazine titled "It's Still Baseball, Cobb!" which insisted on the integrity of the contemporary game. A decade later, however, he and Surface co-authored an article from a different perspective, explaining how "home-run fever" was damaging strategy and actually dampening the excitement of games. He did not think that the overall talent level in the sport had dissipated, but he felt players now approached their work in the wrong way, with too few truly dedicated stars. Aside from Stan Musial and Ted Williams, he refused to believe that any players from later generations could equal the talents of Wagner, Cobb, Ruth, Gehrig, or Foxx, for example.

His two autobiographies, *My Kind of Baseball* (David McKay, 1953) and *My War with Baseball* (Coward-McCann, 1962), sold fairly well and attracted readers with his candid commentary on topics ranging from why "there won't be any more .400 hitters" to "how to get in the doghouse" with management. He railed against the practice of giving large signing bonuses to unproven prospects and identified general managers as the biggest problem in baseball. His conflict with Bill Veeck played a prominent role in both books, which were among the first "tell-all" sports memoirs, although the dirty laundry Hornsby aired regarded differences of baseball opinion, not barroom brawls. Traditionalist baseball fans and gossip-thirsty sportswriters appreciated the older Rajah's candor, but by the time he died, a number of people, including Surface, Veeck, and many of the players Hornsby coached, felt that the former MVP had lost touch with his sport.

In the years following his death, however, testimonials from several generations of observers confirmed that the Rajah's ideas and accomplishments were still respected by some corners of baseball's establishment. His contemporaries Pie Traynor and Specs Toporcer separately stated that Hornsby had been underrated in several aspects of the game, such as baserunning and defense. Offensively, his statistics remained an elusive target for players hoping to make their mark at the plate. In the 1960s, sportswriters routinely used Hornsby's career as a barometer to measure the promise of young hitters (as well as their contentiousness).

One of the most outspoken supporters of Hornsby's singular talent with a bat was a man who received as much if not more praise for his hitting skills than any player in the twentieth century. During spring training in 1938, Hornsby's best offer for a job had come from the owner of a Minneapolis minor league team, whose most promising player was a lanky left fielder named Ted Williams. These two men, whose playing careers abutted one another but did not overlap, covered nearly four decades between them as the most consistent and accomplished batsmen in baseball. The left-handed Williams was openly pleased by comparisons to the greatest right-handed hitter in history. In his memoir *My Turn at Bat* (Simon & Schuster, 1969), Williams remembered that he instantly liked Hornsby in 1938 "because he talked to me"—and because the 42-year-old man regularly bettered the 19-year-old phenom in hitting contests. With a full spring together, the two celebrated batsmen talked about hitting every spare moment, said Williams, "and boy I picked his brains for everything I could." Williams thought Hornsby "was the greatest hitter for average *and* power in the history of baseball," and believed that his sagest advice, which Williams said became his "cardinal rule," was simply "get a good ball to hit."[10]

To a significant extent, Hornsby's peripatetic career, coupled with his obstinacy during and after it, puts his legacy among later generations of baseball players and fans in doubt. By the 1980s and 1990s, the Rajah seemed at times to be just an answer to trivia questions rather than one of the finest players in history. Older fans and serious baseball enthusiasts certainly know his accomplishments and can chuckle at stories of his indelicate exchanges with players, owners, and the baseball commissioner, but to many people, the greatest National League player of his era is just a funny name in the record books.

Although ballplayers themselves are rarely confused with baseball historians, comments from a few major league infielders in recent years illustrate the diminished awareness of Hornsby in the twenty-first century. In 1998, San Francisco Giant Jeff Kent became the first second baseman since the Rajah to achieve multiple seasons with more than 120 RBIs. When asked to comment on the historic accomplishment, Kent "admitted that he never heard of Hornsby."[11] A few years later, Luis Castillo of the Florida Marlins broke Hornsby's record for the longest hitting streak by a second baseman (33 games—Castillo reached 35). Reporters immediately asked him how it felt to surpass such a legendary figure. "Who?" Castillo replied.[12] Finally, Boston Red Sox shortstop Nomar Garciaparra once freely admitted to *Sports Illustrated* writer Michael Bamberger, who was investigating the hitting legacies of Hornsby and Williams, that "I don't know anything about [Hornsby], to tell you the truth."[13] Kent, Castillo, and Garciaparra may not represent the entire major league population, but their evident ignorance of a significant forebear shows that Hornsby's reputation has not lasted in quite the same way that, for example, the reputations of Cobb or Williams have.

Likewise, popular culture has not maintained memories of Hornsby to a large degree, for his story lacks the tragedy of Gehrig's or the political impact of Jackie Robinson's. But Hollywood has given a mention or two to the Rajah in recent years, even if the focus is often on Hornsby's diffidence or his famous habit of wearing out his welcome. His harsh managerial style receives a prominent mention in the most famous quote from the popular 1992 film *A League of Their*

Own. In it, Jimmy Dugan, played by Tom Hanks, is the male manager of an all-female team. He addresses a weeping young woman in the dugout, and informs her: "There's no crying, there's no crying in baseball. Rogers Hornsby was my manager, and he called me a talking pile of pig shit. And that was when my parents drove all the way down from Michigan to see me play the game. And did I cry? No."[14]

Practically the only other notable mention of Hornsby outside sports-oriented publications came in a 1997 *New York Times* article, "Six Degrees of Rogers Hornsby," which extended a marginal Hollywood phenomenon widely enough to incorporate the Rajah. In 1990, playwright John Guare's *Six Degrees of Separation* had premiered with critical acclaim and was subsequently adapted to film. The conceit of Guare's play is that all humans are connected by six or fewer stages of acquaintance. Within a few years, a group of bored and creative college students had adapted the premise into a game in which participants connected actors chosen at random to Kevin Bacon, a performer in an almost countless number of ensemble films, via a chain of co-stars. "Six Degrees of Kevin Bacon" developed a widespread popularity and spawned a book as millions of Americans quizzed each other's knowledge of filmography. Then in 1997, baseball writer Tom Remes produced his own version of the game, organized on the principle that major leaguers have a similar quality of connectedness through their various teammates. In Remes' game, "the center of it all is the greatest right-handed hitter of all-time, Rogers Hornsby." To demonstrate the theory, "Six Degrees of Rogers Hornsby" links more than twenty players active in 1997 to the Rajah, all with less than six common teammates. Although the game was not exhaustively tested, the wealth of connections created by Hornsby's long and well-traveled career seems to make it viable and rather amusing.[15]

Although the general culture has done little to preserve his memory, baseball historians certainly remain aware of the Rajah's accomplishments. The most complete record of Hornsby's life to date is *Rogers Hornsby* (Henry Holt & Company, 1995) by Charles Alexander. Alexander, a professor of history, has written definitive biographies of Ty Cobb and John McGraw and has recently published an excellent book that covers an often overlooked era of baseball, the years of the Great Depression. His examination of the Rajah's life on and off the field is tirelessly researched and written with style. Alexander makes a particular effort to place Hornsby's life in the context of both contemporary baseball and national history. In addition, *Rogers Hornsby* includes thorough detail on Hornsby's family and his later life, subjects that the player had excluded from his own memoirs and that few of his fans and critics had fully known. When the biography was published in 1995—just a year before Hornsby's centennial—

interest in the Rajah resurfaced to some degree because readers of Alexander's book now had a life's worth of context for the weighty statistics and anecdotal conflicts that had previously comprised the whole of the Hornsby story.

Ultimately, though, Rogers Hornsby will be remembered for the two characteristics that inspired his fame in the 1920s: the batting ability that made major league teams covet him and the personality that forced several of those teams to surrender him. The team he managed was victorious in one of the most exciting World Series ever played and he spent more than twenty-three seasons as an active major league player, but the trades and firings that checkered his career sometimes seem most prominent in baseball's memory. When a team trades a superstar for what seems like less than equal value—particularly when that player has been called "difficult," "selfish," or "arrogant"—stories of Hornsby's conflicts with Sam Breadon, William Veeck Sr., or Bill Veeck Jr. are repeated.

As a hitter, Hornsby remains among history's elite, and given the current statistical trends, he will likely keep a few of his records for some time. He is arguably the standard by which batting consistency should be judged; sustaining a batting average better than .400 over five seasons as Hornsby did is a feat unthinkable when no player has reached that benchmark in even one season since 1941. The power of his fluid swing, his ability to drive the ball in all directions, and his renowned awareness of the strike zone helped the Rajah earn his reputation as the finest right-handed hitter in his sport's long history—a designation still applicable more than seventy years since he last played regularly.

Hornsby's philosophy on hitting was as plain and uncomplicated as all his opinions: "You do or you don't," he told Bob Broeg.[16] From the day he shocked Miller Huggins as a suddenly strapping youth in 1916 until his aching feet slowly forced him off the field in the 1930s, from St. Louis to New York to Boston to Chicago and back to St. Louis, Rogers Hornsby simply *did*—as often as any man who ever picked up a bat.

NOTES

1. Bill Surface, "The Last Days of Rogers Hornsby," *Saturday Evening Post*, June 15, 1963, 72.

2. Bob Broeg, "Sports Comment" column, *St. Louis Post-Dispatch*, January 7, 1963, Rogers Hornsby Collection, National Baseball Library, Cooperstown, NY.

3. Surface, "The Last Days of Rogers Hornsby," 72.

4. Ibid., 76.

5. Ibid., 72.

6. Zeke Handler to *Sporting News* editors, unpublished letter, June 1963, Rogers Hornsby Collection, The Sporting News Archives, St. Louis, MO.

7. *Brooklyn Eagle*, October 24, 1945, quoted in Jules Tygiel, *Baseball's Great Experiment: Jackie Robinson and His Legacy* (New York: Oxford University Press, 1997), 77.

8. Frederick Lieb, *Baseball as I Have Known It* (New York: Coward, McCann & Geoghegan, 1977), 57.

9. Alexander, *Rogers Hornsby*, 146–147.

10. Ted Williams, *My Turn at Bat: The Story of My Life* (New York: Simon & Schuster, 1988), 52–53, 63, 118 [originally published 1969].

11. Henry Schulman, "Kent in Range of Team's RBI Record," *San Francisco Chronicle*, July 10, 2000, E5.

12. *Cleveland Plain Dealer*, June 23, 2002, C5.

13. Michael Bamberger, "Hail to the Rajah," *Sports Illustrated*, June 24, 2002, 14.

14. *A League of Their Own*, dir. Penny Marshall (1992; Columbia Tristar Home Entertainment, 1997).

15. Tom Remes, "Six Degrees of Rogers Hornsby," *New York Times*, August 17, 1997, S9.

16. Bob Broeg, *St. Louis Post-Dispatch*, August 21, 1991, 7D.

APPENDIX: ROGERS HORNSBY'S CAREER AND WORLD SERIES STATISTICS

Career Statistics

Year	Club	League	G	AB	R	H	2B	3B	HR	RBI	BA	PO	A	E	FA
1915	St. L. Cardinals	NL	18	57	5	14	2	0	0	4	.246	48	46	8	.922
1916	St. L. Cardinals	NL	139	495	63	155	17	15	6	65	.313	325	315	45	.925
1917	St. L. Cardinals	NL	145	523	86	171	24	17	8	66	.327	268	527	52	.939
1918	St. L. Cardinals	NL	115	416	51	117	19	11	5	60	.281	211	434	46	.967
1919	St. L. Cardinals	NL	138	512	68	163	15	9	8	71	.318	233	367	34	.958
1920	St. L. Cardinals	NL	149	589	96	218	44	20	9	94	.370	343	524	34	.962
1921	St. L. Cardinals	NL	154	592	131	235	44	18	21	126	.397	340	487	27	.944
1922	St. L. Cardinals	NL	154	623	141	250	46	14	42	152	.401	398	473	30	.967
1923	St. L. Cardinals	NL	107	424	89	163	32	10	17	83	.384	323	299	21	.975
1924	St. L. Cardinals	NL	143	536	121	227	43	14	25	94	.424	301	517	30	.965
1925	St. L. Cardinals	NL	138	504	133	203	41	10	39	143	.403	287	416	34	.954
1926	St. L. Cardinals	NL	134	527	96	167	34	5	11	93	.317	245	433	27	.962
1927	N.Y. Giants	NL	155	568	133	205	32	9	26	125	.361	299	582	25	.972
1928	Boston Braves	NL	140	486	99	188	42	7	21	94	.387	295	450	21	.973
1929	Chicago Cubs	NL	156	602	156	229	47	8	39	149	.380	286	547	23	.973
1930	Chicago Cubs	NL	42	104	15	32	5	1	2	18	.308	44	76	11	.916
1931	Chicago Cubs	NL	100	357	64	118	37	1	16	90	.331	128	255	22	.954
1932	Chicago Cubs	NL	19	58	10	13	2	0	1	7	.224	17	10	4	.867
1933	St. L. Cardinals	NL	46	83	9	27	6	0	2	21	.325	24	35	2	.967
1933	St. L. Browns	AL	11	9	2	3	1	0	1	2	.333	0	0	0	.000
	1933 Totals		57	92	11	30	7	0	3	23	.326	24	35	2	.967
1934	St. L. Browns	AL	24	23	2	7	2	0	1	11	.304	2	3	0	1.000

Year	Club		G	AB	R	H	2B	3B	HR	RBI	BA	PO	A	E	FA
1935	St. L. Browns	AL	10	24	1	5	3	0	0	3	.208	38	5	0	1.000
1936	St. L. Browns	AL	2	5	1	2	0	0	0	2	.400	10	0	0	1.000
1937	St. L. Browns	AL	20	56	7	18	3	0	1	11	.321	30	41	4	.947
Major League Totals (23 Seasons)			2259	8173	1579	2930	541	169	301	1584	.358				

A = assists; AB = at-bats; BA = batting average; E = errors; FA = fielding average; G = games; H = hits; HR = home runs; PO = put-outs; R. = runs; RBI = runs batted in; 2B = doubles; 3B = triples

WORLD SERIES STATISTICS

Year	Club	G	AB	R	H	2B	3B	HR	RBI	BA
1926	St. L. Cardinals	7	28	2	7	1	0	0	4	.250
1929	Chicago Cubs	5	21	4	5	1	1	0	1	.238
World Series Totals		12	49	6	12	2	1	0	5	.245

Selected Bibliography

BIOGRAPHIES AND AUTOBIOGRAPHIES OF ROGERS HORNSBY

Alexander, Charles. *Rogers Hornsby*. New York: Henry Holt, 1995.

Hornsby, Rogers. *My Kind of Baseball*. Edited by J. Roy Stockton. New York: David McKay, 1953.

Hornsby, Rogers, and Bill Surface. *My War with Baseball*. New York: Coward-McCann, 1962.

Kavanagh, Jack. *Rogers Hornsby*. New York: Chelsea House Publishers, 1991 (intended for juvenile readers).

BOOKS

Alexander, Charles. *Breaking the Slump: Baseball in the Great Depression*. New York: Columbia University Press, 2002.

———. *John McGraw*. New York: Viking, 1988.

———. *Our Game: An American Baseball History*. New York: Henry Holt, 1991.

———. *Ty Cobb*. New York: Oxford University Press, 1984.

Allen, Lee. *The National League Story*. New York: Hill and Wang, 1961.

Astor, Gerald. *The Baseball Hall of Fame Fiftieth Anniversary Book*. New York: Prentice-Hall, 1988.

Breslin, Jimmy. *Can't Anybody Here Play This Game?* New York: Viking, 1963.

Burk, Robert F. *Never Just a Game: Players, Owners, and American Baseball to 1920*. Chapel Hill: University of North Carolina Press, 1994.

Carter, Craig. *Daguerreotypes*. 8th ed. St. Louis: The Sporting News, 1990.

Cobb, Ty, and Al Stump. *My Life in Baseball: The True Record*. New York: Doubleday, 1961.

Cohen, Richard M., and David S. Neft. *The World Series: Complete Play-by-Play of Every Game, 1903–1989*. New York: Macmillan, 1990.

Curran, William. *Big Sticks: The Batting Revolution of the Twenties*. New York: William Morrow, 1990.

Daley, Arthur. *Kings of the Home Run*. New York: Putnam, 1962.

Dickey, Glenn. *The History of American League Baseball Since 1901*. New York: Stein & Day, 1980.

———. *The History of National League Baseball Since 1876*. New York: Stein & Day, 1982.

Enright, Jim. *The Chicago Cubs*. New York: Macmillan, 1975.

Ginsburg, Daniel E. *The Fix Is In: A History of Baseball Gambling and Game Fixing Scandals*. Jefferson, NC: McFarland & Co., 1995.

Golenbock, Peter. *The Spirit of St. Louis: A History of the St. Louis Cardinals and Browns*. New York: Spike, 2000.

———. *Wrigleyville: A Magical History Tour of the Chicago Cubs*. New York: St. Martin's, 1996.

Hornsby, Rogers, et al. *Secrets of Baseball Told by the Greatest Old-Timers*. Bedford, MA: Applewood Books, 1996.

James, Bill. *The Bill James Guide to Baseball Managers from 1870 to Today*. New York: Scribner, 1997.

———. *The New Bill James Historical Baseball Abstract*. New York: Free Press, 2001.

Kashatus, William C. *Connie Mack's '29 Triumph: The Rise and Fall of the Philadelphia Athletics Dynasty*. Jefferson, NC: McFarland & Co., 1999.

Kavanagh, Jack. *Ol' Pete: The Grover Cleveland Alexander Story*. South Bend, IN: Diamond Communications, 1996.

Lieb, Frederick G. *Baseball as I Have Known It*. New York: Coward, McCann & Geoghegan, 1977.

———. *The St. Louis Cardinals: The Story of a Great Baseball Club*. Carbondale, IL: Southern Illinois University Press, 2001 [originally published 1945].

Mann, Arthur. *Branch Rickey: American in Action*. Boston: Houghton Mifflin, 1957.

Murdock, Eugene. *Baseball Players and Their Times: Oral Histories of the Game, 1920–1940*. Westport, CT: Meckler, 1991.

Neyer, Rob. *Rob Neyer's Big Book of Baseball Lineups: A Complete Guide to the Best, Worst, and Most Memorable Players to Ever Grace the Major Leagues*. New York: Fireside Books, 2003.

Parker, Clifton Blue. *Fouled Away: The Baseball Tragedy of Hack Wilson*. Jefferson, NC: McFarland & Co., 2000.

Pietrusza, David. *Judge and Jury: The Life and Times of Judge Kenesaw Mountain Landis*. South Bend, IN: Diamond Communications, 1998.

Polner, Murray. *Branch Rickey: A Biography*. New York: Atheneum, 1982.

Smith, Curt. *Storied Stadiums: Baseball's History Through Its Ballparks*. New York: Carroll & Graf, 2001.

Sullivan, George. *Sluggers: Twenty-Seven of Baseball's Greatest*. New York: Atheneum, 1991.

Tygiel, Jules. *Baseball's Great Experiment: Jackie Robinson and His Legacy*. New York: Oxford University Press, 1997.

Veeck, Bill, and Ed Linn. *Veeck As in Wreck: The Autobiography of Bill Veeck*. Chicago: University of Chicago Press, 2001 [originally published 1962].

Ward, Geoffrey C., and Ken Burns. *Baseball: An Illustrated History*. New York: Alfred A. Knopf, 1994.

Williams, Ted, with Jim Prime. *Ted Williams' Hit List*. Indianapolis: Master's Press, 1996.

Williams, Ted, and John Underwood. *My Turn at Bat: The Story of My Life*. New York: Simon & Schuster, 1988 [originally published 1969].

———. *The Science of Hitting*. New York: Simon & Schuster, 1986.

ARTICLES

Bamberger, Michael. "Hail to the Rajah." *Sports Illustrated*, June 24, 2002.

Birtwell, Roger. "Traynor Claims Baseball's Rajah Under-rated." *Boston Globe*, July 15, 1969.

Breit, Harvey. "Mister Baseball Starts His Second Career." *New York Times Magazine*, May 11, 1952.

Broeg, Bob. "Mr. Blunt: The One and Only Rogers Hornsby." *Sporting News*, February 22, 1969.

———. "The Rog Wore Nobody's Collar." *St. Louis Post-Dispatch*, February 18, 1978.

Cobb, Ty. "They Don't Play Baseball Any More." *Life*, March 17, 1952.

Colver, J. Newton. "Hornsby the Greatest Batter of All Time." *Baseball Magazine*, October 1927.

Conlin, Bill. "Hornsby Pitchers' Friend Now." *Baseball Digest*, July 1951.

Crusinberry, James. "Rogers Hornsby, Non-Stop Man of Baseball." *Baseball Magazine*, May 1951.

Drebinger, John. "Rogers Hornsby—Star of the Cubs." *New York Times*, September 27, 1929.

Frick, Ford, and Frank Graham. "Baseball's Greatest Dramas: Alex Fans Lazzeri." *New York Journal-American*, March 21, 1961.

Graham, Frank. "Hail the Prodigal Rajah!" *Sport*, March 1952.

"Hard-Boiled Hornsby Starts in on the Browns." *Life*, March 31, 1952.

Hornsby, Rogers. "How to Get Fired." *Look*, July 14, 1953.

Hornsby, Rogers, and Bill Surface. "What Home-Run Fever Is Doing to Baseball." *This Week Magazine*, March 25, 1962.

———. "You've Got to Cheat to Win in Baseball." *True*, August 1961.

Hornsby, Rogers, and Bill van Fleet. "My Biggest Baseball Day." *Chicago Daily News*, March 1943.

Hornsby, Rogers, and Tim Cohane. "It's Still Baseball, Cobb!" *Look*, June 17, 1952.

Keener, Sid. "Scout Paid $500 for Raw-Kid Hornsby." *Sporting News*, October 24, 1951.

Lane, Franklin C. "The Amazing Hornsby Deal." *Baseball Magazine*, March 1928.

———. "The Greatest Player in the National League." *Baseball Magazine*, May 1930.

———. "Handicapping Baseball's Greatest Hitter." *Baseball Magazine*, March 1925.

———. "Hornsby Moves On." *Baseball Magazine*, January 1929.

———. "Hornsby's Winning System." *Baseball Magazine*, November 1926.

———. "The Last of the Field Leaders." *Baseball Magazine*, July 1931.

———. "The Passing of Rogers Hornsby." *Baseball Magazine*, October 1932.

Lipsyte, Robert. "A Met for One Season." *New York Times*, June 16, 1969.

———. "Rajah's Return." *New York Times Magazine*, April 29, 1962.

Mann, Arthur. "New York's New Babe Ruth." 10 parts. *New York Evening World*, January 11–20, 1927.

Mason, Ward. "The Star of the 1916 Recruits." *Baseball Magazine*, October 1916.

"Rajah Deposed." *Time*, June 23, 1952.

Remes, Tom. "Six Degrees of Rogers Hornsby." *New York Times*, August 17, 1997.

Sher, Jack. "Rogers Hornsby: The Mighty Rajah." *Sport*, July 1949.

Spink, J. G. Taylor. "The Strange Story of Rogers Hornsby." In *Baseball Register*. Edited by J. G. Taylor Spink, Paul A. Rickart, and Joe Abramovich. St. Louis: The Sporting News, 1954, 3–13.

Stockton, J. Roy. "Can the Rajah Rejuvenate the Browns?" *Saturday Evening Post*, February 9, 1952.

———. "No Clowns on Browns with Hornsby at Helm." *Sporting News*, October 17, 1951.

———. "Rajah Stymied in Comeback." *Baseball Digest*, January 1951.

Stull, Dorothy. "Subject: Rogers Hornsby." *Sports Illustrated*, September 10, 1956.

Surface, Bill. "The Last Days of Rogers Hornsby." *Saturday Evening Post*, June 15, 1963.

Toporcer, George. "The Greatest Hitter of All Time." *Baseball Bluebook*, May 1953.

STATISTICAL REFERENCES

Baseball Encyclopedia: The Complete and Definitive Record of Major League Baseball, The. 10th ed. New York: Macmillan, 1996.

BaseballLibrary.com. www.baseballlibrary.com.

Baseball-Reference.com. www.baseball-reference.com.

Neft, David S., Richard M. Cohen, and Michael L. Neft. *The Sports Encyclopedia: Baseball 2004*. New York: St. Martin's, 2004.

Selected Bibliography

COLLECTIONS

Branch Rickey Collection. The Sporting News Archives. St. Louis.
John McGraw Collection. National Baseball Library. Cooperstown, NY.
Grover Cleveland Alexander Collection. National Baseball Library. Cooperstown, NY.
Rogers Hornsby Collection. National Baseball Library. Cooperstown, NY.
Rogers Hornsby Collection. The Sporting News Archives. St. Louis.

INDEX

About the Author

JONATHAN D'AMORE is a freelance writer living in Chapel Hill, North Carolina. He has worked closely with the authors of several literary biographies, and his interviews and articles have appeared in a number of publications, including the *Carolina Quarterly*.